styling

web pages

with CSS

Visual QuickProject Guide

by Tom Negrino and Dori Smith

Peachpit Press

Visual QuickProject Guide
Styling Web Pages with CSS
Tom Negrino and Dori Smith

Peachpit Press

1249 Eighth Street
Berkeley, CA 94710
510/524-2178
510/524-2221 (fax)

Find us on the Web at: www.peachpit.com
To report errors, please send a note to errata@peachpit.com
Peachpit Press is a division of Pearson Education

Editor: Nancy Davis
Production: Becky Winter
Compositor: David Van Ness
Cover design: Peachpit Press, Aren Howell
Cover production: Mike Tanamachi
Cover photo credit: Juho Kuva / iStock image
Interior design: Elizabeth Castro
Indexer: Emily Glossbrenner, FireCrystal Communications

ISBN 13: 978-0-321-55557-1
ISBN 10:   0-321-55557-0

9 8 7 6 5 4 3 2 1

Printed and bound in the United States of America

To Nancy Davis,
our beloved editor and friend, for
making our work better (way better!)
for more than a decade.

And in memoriam to
Nancy's editing partner,
Emma Mingus Davis Hack,
1991–2008.

contents

contents

introduction

The Visual QuickProject Guide that you hold in your hands offers a unique way to learn about new technologies. Instead of drowning you in theoretical possibilities and lengthy explanations, this Visual QuickProject Guide uses big, color illustrations coupled with clear, concise step-by-step instructions to show you how to complete one specific project in a matter of hours.

Our project in this book is to create a compelling, standards-compliant Web site using Cascading Style Sheets (CSS). We'll use CSS in two main ways; first, we'll use it for page layout, placing all of the text and images just where we want them on our pages. Then, we'll use CSS to style the text, giving it the look we need for maximum impact. Along the way, you'll also learn how to create CSS to wrap text around images; create menus and navigation bars; and how you can change the entire look of your site by changing just one file. By the time you're finished with this book, you'll have a good grounding in CSS that you can apply to your own projects and Web sites.

This book covers the basics of CSS, but it doesn't presume to teach you all about Web development; no book of this size can fully cover such a large subject. Before you dive into CSS, you should already know how to create HTML markup and save it as a Web page and how to upload that page to a Web server so that it is accessible in a Web browser. You don't need to be an expert XHTML jockey, but you should be familiar with the basic XHTML tags and the fundamental structure of an XHTML page.

what you'll create

We will build a Web site for a fictional business, Alpaca Repo. This business, if it really existed, would repossess these lovable, goofy-looking animals from owners that had fallen behind on their payments. We hasten to add that we personally would never tow away an alpaca, and no alpacas were harmed in the making of this book. Because the Web site we'll create showcases all the basic techniques, you'll be able to use what you learn to create or update your own Web site, whether it's your personal Web site or an updated site for your company or organization.

In the past, it was common to lay out the elements on a Web page using XHTML tables. Text and images were placed in cells of the table. To style text on the page, you added XHTML style tags to each bit of text. These techniques are obsolete, and no modern site should use them. Instead, this book will cover how to create a modern looking site, using CSS to lay out the page elements and control the appearance of the elements on the page.

how web pages work

A modern Web page is made up of a number of files. These files are put together, or rendered, by the Web browser, which displays the page to the viewer. Several files make up a Web page:

- The XHTML file contains the readable content of the page, i.e., the page's text. An XHTML file is required. This file also contains some basic information about how you want the browser to understand the page.

- The Cascading Style Sheet holds rules about the presentation of the content. These can be instructions for the layout of the content on the page, or instructions on how the text is to be styled. A CSS file is not, strictly speaking, required, but without one, your page will look awfully dull.

- The JavaScript file has the scripts that add behaviors and user interaction to the page. This can be anything from a simple form validation that makes sure the user has filled in a form properly, to complex Web-based applications that rival desktop applications. Again, a JavaScript file isn't required.

- Most pages have one or more graphic images that add interest to the page.

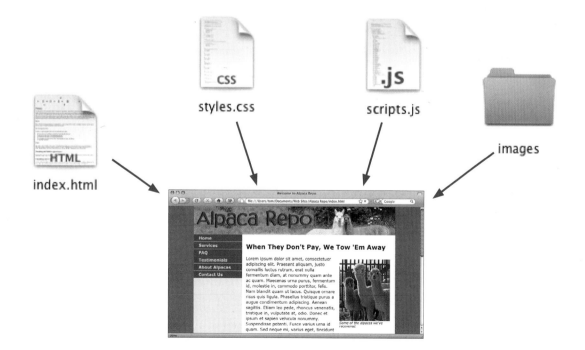

styles.css

scripts.js

images

index.html

how this book works

The title of each section explains what is covered on that page.

Numbered steps explain actions to perform in a specific order.

Code blocks show what should be put in the various XHTML and CSS files.

Captions explain what you're doing and why. They also point to terms of interest.

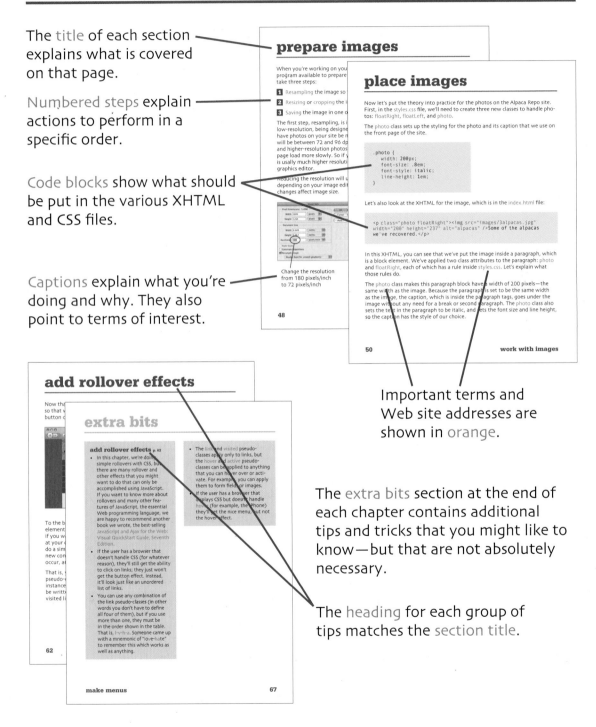

Important terms and Web site addresses are shown in orange.

The extra bits section at the end of each chapter contains additional tips and tricks that you might like to know—but that are not absolutely necessary.

The heading for each group of tips matches the section title.

useful tools

You'll need a few tools in order to write CSS and HTML. The most important program to have is a text editor. We like ones that are designed to be used by programmers, because they have the ability to color different parts of the code, which makes the code easier to read and work with. On the Macintosh, we recommend BBEdit or the free TextWrangler (shown). On Windows, Notepad is acceptable. You can also use a WYSIWYG (What You See Is What You Get) Web editor, such as Dreamweaver. Your choice of tool is actually not that important, as long as it can create plain text files. We don't recommend the use of a word processor, such as Microsoft Word. A Word document is not a plain text file, and though you can make Word output plain text, it's too easy to forget and accidentally save in Word format.

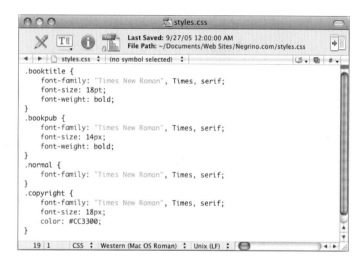

Of course, you'll also need Web browsers to view your work, both locally and on the Web. Different browsers can render CSS-based pages differently, so if you're going to get serious about CSS development, it's a good idea to have all of the following browsers available for testing. There are only four browsers you need to worry about, because they cover the vast majority of Web users. On Windows, you need Internet Explorer 7 or later and Firefox. On the Mac, it's Safari (this will also cover iPhone users) and Firefox.

Finally, if your site is on a hosted server (most are), you'll need an FTP (File Transfer Protocol) program to upload the files you create from your computer to the Web server. Popular FTP programs on the Mac include Cyberduck, Transmit, and Fetch, and on Windows, CuteFTP, SmartFTP, and Filezilla. Dreamweaver and many other WYSIWYG programs have built-in FTP tools.

the next step

While this Visual QuickProject Guide will walk you through the steps required to lay out and style your Web pages using CSS, there's much more to learn about XHTML and CSS. After you complete your QuickProject, consider picking up a couple of other books as an in-depth, handy reference.

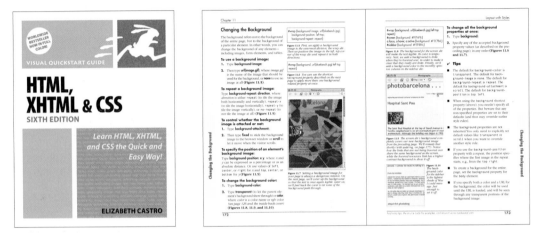

To delve deeper into XHTML and CSS, check out HTML, XHTML & CSS: Visual QuickStart Guide, 6th Edition, by Elizabeth Castro. This book gives you a fine overview and reference.

For a closer look at just CSS, we recommend Stylin' with CSS: A Designer's Guide, Second Edition, by Charles Wyke-Smith.

Both books give you clear examples, concise, step-by-step instructions, and many tips that will help you improve your Web sites.

1. introducing css

When you first began working with XHTML (We're going to refer to XHTML in this book, but if you want to substitute "HTML" in your head, it's fine with us; we're not purists), you learned that you use it to define the structure of your Web page document, and to define the nature of each element of your page's content. By adding markup to an element, you are telling the Web browser what that bit of content is. Markup is made up of tags, and tag names are enclosed in angle brackets. For example, you define a bit of text as a paragraph by surrounding it with the <p> and </p> tags, like so:

<p>Alpaca wool is prized for its beauty and softness.</p>

Marking up text into paragraphs provides some structure to the document, and adding section headings helps define further what text is important. You define headings by containing the heading text with heading tags:

<h1>Our selection of repossessed alpacas</h1>

Some tags for content that isn't text (like an image) use a single tag (there's no closing tag):

<img src="images/alpaca.jpg" alt="a fine looking alpaca" />

XHTML provides the structure of the document; CSS defines the presentation of the content, telling the Web browser how it should display the content to the user. For example, you use CSS to define the font of the text on the page, and where the text appears on the page.

In this chapter, we'll delve into what you need to write CSS and explain the basic structures of CSS, including rules, classes, and IDs. We'll also learn about inline styles, internal stylesheets, and external stylesheets. Finally, we'll touch on the cascade, the idea that lends Cascading Style Sheets their power. It's a lot to cover, but we'll make it easy. Let's go!

choose your tools

The good news about writing CSS is that you don't need any special software to create it. All you need is a text editor, and the ones included with Windows and Mac OS X will do. On Windows, that's Notepad, and on the Mac, TextEdit will work just fine. What is important is that you save the CSS file as a plain text file (and add a .css file extension to the filename). You'll also probably need an FTP program to upload your CSS and XHTML files to your Web server.

You can get away with using these simple text editors, but if you'll be writing a lot of CSS, it will be well worth the expense to purchase a program that is designed as a specific CSS editor. These programs help you in many ways, including automatically building the CSS code from choices you make in panels or dialog boxes, ensuring that you're not frustrated because you made a typo. Most of them have built-in previewing features, which let you instantly see the effects of your changes without having to switch to a Web browser. And the better programs have debugging and validation features that help you fix any problems that crop up. Here are a couple of favorite CSS editors that we can confidently recommend. Both have free trial versions you can download.

If you work on both Windows and Mac, check out WesternCiv's Style Master (www.westciv.com).

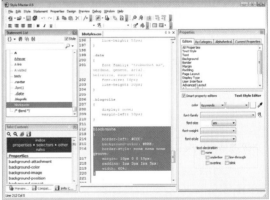

If you're Mac-based, take a look at MacRabbit's CSSEdit (www.macrabbit.com).

create a stylesheet

No matter what program you use to create your CSS, all you need to do to get started is to launch the program, which will create a new document. Then immediately save it onto your hard disk, using the name styles.css. In the next section, we'll begin writing a CSS rule and filling in that blank space.

write css rules

A CSS rule consists of instructions that apply to one or more elements in your document. A rule has two parts: the selector and the declaration block.

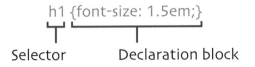

This rule sets the contents of any h1 tags in the document to be 1.5 ems in size. Here's how the rule looks in action:

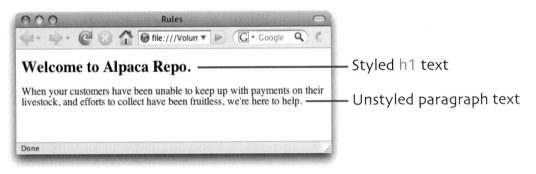

The selector part of the rule defines what the rule applies to and can be any XHTML tag, as well as other CSS elements, such as classes and IDs (we'll get to those later in this chapter). The declaration block defines what the rule does, and includes everything between and including the curly braces.

The declaration block opens with the left brace, then the declaration itself begins. It includes a property (in the rule above, that's font-size); a colon; and a value for the property (1.5em above). A property is always paired with a value. After the value, there must be a semicolon (indicating the end of the declaration). Within a single declaration block, you can have as many declarations as you want, as long as they are separated by semicolons, as shown below. Finally, you close the declaration block with a right brace.

h1 {font-size: 1.5em; font-weight: bold; color: green;}

The spaces after the colon and semicolon within the declaration are optional, but makes it a bit easier to read your rules, so we recommend it. You don't need a space between the final semicolon and the right brace.

You can also write the rule with returns and indentations between each declaration, which can make the rule easier to read, like so:

```
h1 {
    font-size: 1.5em;
    font-weight: bold;
    color: green;
}
```

If you want to apply the same declarations to multiple selectors, just add the additional selectors to the rule, separated by commas:

```
h1, h2, h3 {font-weight: bold; color: green;}
```

This can save you a lot of typing, because you don't have to repeat the declarations for each tag. In this case, removing the font-size declaration makes sense, because the different heading levels have inherent sizes. The rule above makes all three heading sizes bold and green.

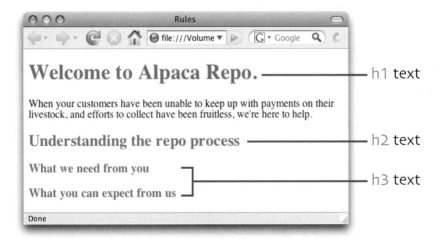

create a class

You use a tag selector when you want to apply a style rule to all of the instances of that tag. For example, if you define a rule for the <p> tag, that rule will be applied to the contents of every <p> in your document. If you're using external stylesheets (more about those later in this chapter), the rule will be applied to every <p> in your whole site. But what if you have some paragraphs that you want to treat differently? They're still paragraphs, but you need some way to identify them for special treatment. That's what a CSS class does. There are two things you need to do to use a class in your documents. In the XHTML markup, you add a class attribute to the tag, like so (for clarity, we haven't included all the paragraph text in the line below):

```
<p class="bodytext">When your customers...</p>
```

You must also add a style rule in the CSS stylesheet:

```
.bodytext {font-family: Arial, Helvetica, sans-serif;}
```

Notice that the class name in the CSS stylesheet is preceded by a period (.). The period is required in the stylesheet, but it's not used in the XHTML. The result of the rule looks like this:

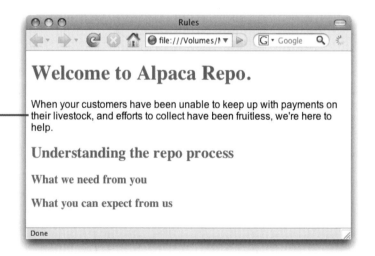

A class can be applied to more than one element; in fact, that's usually the case. Use a class when you want to reuse a style rule in more than one place in your document or throughout your site. The elements don't have to be the same, either; you could, for example, apply the same class style rule to headings and paragraphs.

introducing css

define an id

Classes let you target one or more elements on your page, but if you need to be more specific, you can use an ID. Unlike classes, IDs must be unique within an XHTML document. You can, however, use the same ID name in more than one page of your site, as long as there is only one instance of the ID in each document.

Again, you'll need to add to your XHTML markup and also add a style rule in your CSS stylesheet. Begin by adding the markup, like so (because a copyright notice is only likely to appear once on a page, it's a good candidate for an ID):

`< p id = "copyright" > Copyright 2008 Alpaca Repo, Inc. All rights reserved. < /p >`

The style rule looks like this:

`# copyright {color: gray; font-style: italic; text-align: center;}`

Notice that in the stylesheet, the ID name is preceded by the hash mark (#), but the hash mark does not appear in the XHTML. The result of applying the ID selector rule looks like this:

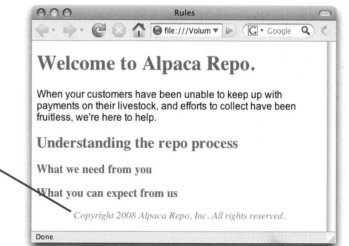

When you name the ID, be sure that you use only letters and numbers, with the caveat that the first character cannot be a number. So #body2 is acceptable, but #2body is not. You can also use underscores in an ID name, but not spaces. The same naming rules also apply to classes.

comment your css

One of the best gifts you can give to yourself is to add comments to your CSS as you write it. It's very easy to write a stylesheet and create class and ID names that make perfect sense in the moment. But when you go back to modify some styles six months later, you may not remember the difference between .content and .content2. Adding comments while you're creating the style will pay off down the line.

To add a comment to your CSS stylesheet, type /* at the beginning of the comment and */ at the end, enclosing the comment in between, like so:

/* This is the style for names of the authors */

.byline {style declaration goes here}

Note that CSS comments are different from XHTML comments, which begin with < !-- and end with -->.

You can also "comment out" part of a style rule, which is useful when you are making changes and testing your CSS. Here is what that looks like; we're using the vertical way of writing the style rule for clarity.

```
h1, h2, h3 {
    color: green;
    /* font-weight: bold; */
}
```

using internal styles

A few pages back, we asked you to create a stylesheet document in whatever program you are using. By doing that, you created an external stylesheet, that is, a document that contains only CSS rules. That's the recommended way to use CSS, and we'll go into external stylesheets in more detail in the next section.

There are two other ways to write style rules: inline and embedded. An inline style is added to an XHTML tag, using the style attribute, like this:

```
<p>This is the default paragraph style.</p>
<p style="color: blue; font-size: 1.5em; font-style: italic;">Here I've added an inline style rule.</p>
```

This is the result:

Embedded styles go in the head of your XHTML document, between the <head> and </head> tags. You enclose the style rules in <style> tags, like this:

```
<head>
    <style type="text/css">
    h1, h2, h3 {
        color: green;
        font-weight: bold;
    }
    .bodytext {
        font-family: Arial, Helvetica, sans-serif;
    }
    </style>
</head>
```

Inline and embedded styles work only for the tag and the page that they are on, respectively. That's why we don't think you should use inline styles at all, and think you should only use embedded styles for testing. It's much better to have your styles in an external stylesheet, because that way all the pages in your site can share the styles.

use external stylesheets

By putting your styles in a separate document, some or all of the pages in your site can link to the stylesheet, sharing its style rules. When you want to change the look of your site, you just edit the style rules in the external sheet, and the changes automatically ripple throughout your site. Instead of changing dozens or hundreds of pages, you just have to modify one. It's a tremendous time saver.

There are two ways to connect your XHTML documents to your CSS stylesheet: linking and importing. The former is a simple <link> to the stylesheet; the browser knows to then get styles from the link's target and apply them to each XHTML page as it is loaded. Most of the time, linking is all you need. The @import style rule is more flexible, because you can not only bring styles from an external stylesheet into an XHTML document, but you can also import one or more CSS files into another. With larger sites, this allows you to further organize the style rules into easily understandable documents.

forumstyles.css   styles.css   index.html

In this example, styles in forumstyles.css are imported into styles.css, and the styles in both are then linked to index.html.

To create a link from an XHTML document to an external stylesheet, add the <link> tag in the <head> tags, like this:

```
<head>
    <link href="styles.css" type="text/css" rel="stylesheet" media="screen" />
</head>
```

In the <link> tag, the href attribute specifies the stylesheet's location; the type attribute alerts the browser that the file contains CSS; the rel attribute tells the browser that this link will be a stylesheet; and the media attribute specifies the media type. In this case, it says the stylesheet should be used for display in a Web browser, but if the attribute was "print" the stylesheet would contain print-friendly styles that you developed. Similarly, if the attribute was "hand-held" the stylesheet would contain styles you had optimized for mobile devices.

To import a stylesheet into an XHTML document, add a <style> tag to the head of the document, as we did in "Using Internal Styles," earlier in this chapter, then add @import url(yourfilename.css); like this:

```
<head>
    <style type="text/css">
        @import url(styles.css);
    </style>
</head>
```

An external stylesheet can include as many @import style rules as you want. This allows you to virtually consolidate multiple stylesheets into a single sheet which contains only @import rules (in effect creating a "master" stylesheet), then link that master sheet to all of your XHTML documents. As an example, imagine that you have one stylesheet that contains all the rules for how text in your site will be presented (text.css); another with all the layout rules (layout.css); and a third with styles for the navigation bar (navbar.css). Then you import all of these into the "master" stylesheet (masterstyles.css). That stylesheet only contains this:

```
@import url(text.css);
@import url(layout.css);
@import url(navbar.css);
```

In each of your XHTML documents, add a link tag to the "master" sheet as described previously (using a link instead of an import works around a problem with Internet Explorer), like this:

```
<head>
    <link href="masterstyles.css" type="text/css" rel="stylesheet"
      media="screen" />
</head>
```

Now you can add or subtract stylesheets to and from your site simply by changing the @import rules in masterstyles.css.

An embedded stylesheet can import styles and also include other style rules. However, the @import rule(s) must come first.

understand the cascade

When you're working with CSS, it's important to know that the placement of style rules within the stylesheets and XHTML will affect the way those rules will be applied when the browser builds the page. Because style rules can reside in several different places, you could have conflicts between styles affecting a particular element. For example, different rules styling the <p> tag could be in both an external stylesheet and embedded in the XHTML page. There needs to be a method of resolving these conflicts, and that's what the cascade is: rules that determine which conflicting rules win out and what gets displayed.

The cascade can get quite complex, but it can be boiled down into two main rules:

1. The closer a rule is to the content being styled, the higher its precedence.

2. The most specific rule wins.

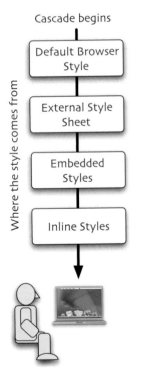

Cascade begins

Default Browser Style

External Style Sheet

Embedded Styles

Inline Styles

Where the style comes from

First, let's talk about the order of precedence for styles. All browsers have a built-in default stylesheet that displays XHTML elements if there are no CSS stylesheets present. These are overridden by rules in any external stylesheets. Within the XHTML document, embedded styles are next in the preference order. And finally, inline styles—the ones closest to the content—win out.

Next up is specificity. The order here can be complex, but almost all the time, all you have to remember is this: when applied to the same elements, ID selectors override class selectors, which in turn trump tag selectors.

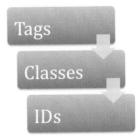

Tags

Classes

IDs

extra bits

choose your tools p. 2

- You might also consider tools that are both CSS and HTML editors. On Windows, Newsgator's TopStyle is popular (www.newsgator.com). On the Mac, Panic's Coda is a good choice (www.panic.com).

write css rules p. 4

- CSS is very picky and unforgiving with typos and capitalization. For example, if you leave out a semicolon, the entire rule may be ignored. The exception is the very last declaration inside a declaration block; for that one, the semicolon is optional. We recommend that you include it anyway; it doesn't hurt, and it's better to get into the habit of always putting it in.

- Don't forget the period before class names, either. If you do, the rule will be ignored.

- In CSS, you must always use straight quotes, ("), not curly quotes (" "). Curly quotes are sometimes called typographer's quotes or smart quotes.

create a class p. 6

- There are ways to get much more specific about the elements you are targeting with a class. We'll dive into those methods in Chapter 6, "Targeting Your Styles."

- Don't go crazy with classes. Create as many as you need, but not more than you need. Think about your document and the styles it needs to have, then create the minimum number of style rules to accomplish your goal. What you don't want to have is a unique class or ID for every different tag in your markup. Too many classes and IDs will make things difficult and confusing when you go to change styles later.

- Don't name styles with names like .big_red_font, because when you change the style later, it won't make sense anymore. Instead, use meaningful style names that describe the purpose of the style, like #footer or .caption.

extra bits

define an id p. 7

- Here's a tip for remembering how to differentiate between IDs and classes: an ID must be unique, that is, there can be one and only one of a given ID on a page. One is a number, so we put the number sign (#) on the ID.

- You can name a class and an ID identically, but we don't recommend it, as it will sooner or later lead to confusion.

- IDs are also used to target specific elements to be manipulated by Web browsers' scripting language, JavaScript.

understand the cascade p. 12

- There is actually one more level of styling between the default browser styles and external styles, called user styles. All browsers allow users to create local stylesheets that, if desired, can be set to override all other styles. The reason we didn't mention it before is that most people simply don't use this capability. It's mainly used by people with disabilities, such as poor eyesight. Those folks can create a user stylesheet that makes all text larger and therefore easier to read.

2. layout and positioning

One of the first decisions you will have to make about your site is its layout. How many columns will your site have? Does it have a header and a footer? Consider sketching out a layout on a piece of paper, or even creating a mockup in a graphics program. In this chapter, you'll see how you can use <div> XHTML tags and CSS rules to define the different areas on the page. In the figure on this page, we've shown the divs, labelled with the CSS class name for each.

When you begin working on your site, we suggest that you start by creating the most important part of the site: its content. Write (or collect from coworkers) the site's copy, and gather the images. Make sure that the images are in the correct format for the Web, either JPEG, PNG, or GIF. If you don't have the site's text yet, you can always add in sample text ("The quick brown fox...").

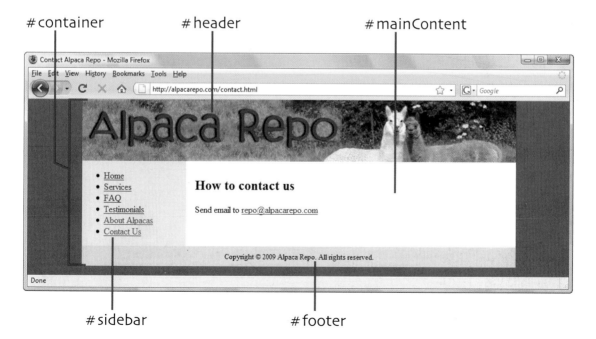

block vs inline tags

Before we jump into creating the layout, you need to know a few more things about XHTML. Much of XHTML can be separated into two types of tags: block tags and inline tags. For instance, all the heading tags are block elements; that is, if you put something in an < h1 > there will automatically be a line break after the < /h1 >. Other common block tags are < p > and < blockquote >.

Inline tags are usually used to style text within a line and don't cause a line break. Common inline tags include < i >, < em >, < strong >, and < b >.

Two tags, < div > (a block tag) and < span > (an inline tag), are specifically meant to be containers, to help add structure to your page.

It's considered good practice to use as few div and span tags as possible. If your markup is meaningful—that is, your paragraphs are inside < p > tags, your headings are inside < h# > tags, and so on—you don't need as many of them. For instance, you never need a div around paragraphs or headings, because those are already block elements.

A series of divs on your page, with rules that specify their position, make up your page's layout. In this example, we've shown a page from Alpaca Repo in Dreamweaver, with its option to show all the divs in different colors turned on to make the divs easier to see.

　　　　　　　　　　　　layout and positioning

the box model

Every block element is a rectangular block (like a box), and that box is made up of parts that you can use CSS to address and manipulate. By default, the borders of the boxes are not visible, and the background is transparent, so you don't actually see the boxes, but trust us, they're there.

When working with CSS and layout, you're creating boxes (sometimes by adding a div) and positioning them on your pages. Each box contains several properties: its margin (the distance between the box and other elements), border (the line that defines the outside of the box), padding (the distance of a box's content from its border), and content (the text or images—or other boxes—that are inside the box).

Using CSS, you can set rules for each of these elements. For example, you can set different rules for the top, right, bottom, and left sides of an element.

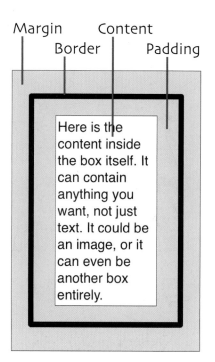

The margin, border, and padding properties allow you to set values for each of the four sides individually or jointly. In other words it's perfectly okay to write a rule in different ways (we're styling a class named #theDiv just as an example):

```
#theDiv { margin: 10px; }

#theDiv { margin-top: 10px; margin-right: 10px;
          margin-bottom: 10px; margin-left: 10px; }

#theDiv { margin: 10px 10px 10px 10px; }

#theDiv { margin: 10px 10px; }
```

Each of these rules does the same thing: applies a 10 pixel margin around #theDiv. When a property such as margin is given a single value (the first rule

the box model (cont.)

above), it's applied to all four sides. In the second rule, each side is individually specified. When it's given four values, as in the third rule, they are applied to the top, right, bottom, and left, respectively (think about a clock face, and go around in a clockwise manner starting at 12 and going to 3, 6, and 9 to remember this). When a property is given two values, as in the last rule, the first value is applied to the top and bottom, and the second value goes to the left and right. If a value for a property is zero, there is no need to give it a unit of measurement, as zero is zero whether it's in pixels or points.

You apply the padding property in the same way as you apply margin.

The border property has three associated properties: width, style, and color. Say that you want a thin black line above and below your text. You can set the border around your text (that is, you would create a rule for the tag that contains your text) to 1px solid black just for the top and bottom. If you don't set the other sides, they'll be set to 0 by default.

```
.lines {
    border-top: 1px solid black;
    border-bottom: 1px solid black;
}
```

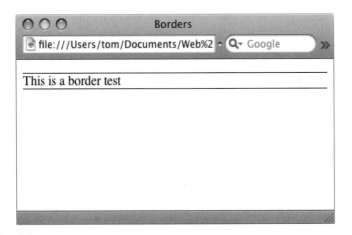

The border-width can be set in any unit (ems, pixels, or percent). The border-style can be set to none, hidden, solid, dotted, dashed, double, groove, ridge, inset, or outset. Some of these look terrible, so use them with care. You can set border-color using color names or other methods (see the extra bits for more detail).

positioning boxes

After you have created your boxes, you want to place them on your page. In order to do that you need to understand the different ways CSS can position block elements. In the examples in this section, we've turned on a thin green border around the divs on the page, so that you can tell where they are.

Static positioning means that the box ends up where it would normally end up, all on its own. Each element is laid out one after the other. The margin settings for each box determine the amount of space between them. Static positioning is the default.

Relative positioning is just like static except that you can set its left and top positions. The positioning is relative to the original position of the element, not relative to any other element on the page. In this example, we've pushed the alpaca picture 80 pixels down and to the right. You can see how it impinges on the other divs but still takes up all the vertical space that it did originally.

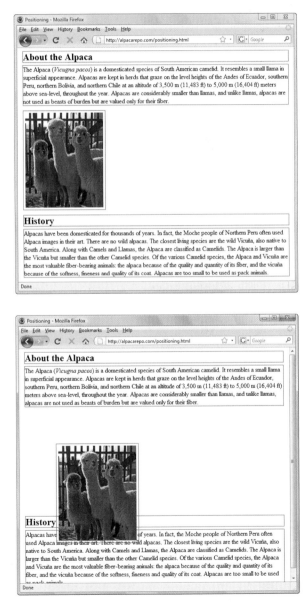

positioning boxes (cont.)

Absolute positioning places an element in reference to its container. If you have an absolutely positioned box placed 100 pixels from the top of the page, and another absolutely positioned box inside that box that is also set to be 100 pixels down, the interior box will be 200 pixels down from the top of the page, not 100—because its frame of reference is to the box that it is inside. In this example, absolute positioning takes the picture out of the flow, because it is now 80 pixels down and to the right of the top-left corner of the page.

Fixed positioning, on the other hand, is based on the page itself. If you set a box to be fixed at 100 pixels down, it will always be there, even if you scroll the page. When you scroll, that box will move down with you so that it's always 100 pixels down from the top of the visible page.

understand float

When you want a box to stick to one side or the other of its container (imagine positioning a photo inside a column), you need to float the box. The values for float are left, right, none, and inherit.

Left: a box that is floated to the left causes everything else on the page (well, everything that isn't explicitly told to be somewhere else) to wrap around it to the right.

Right: just like left, a box floated to the right causes everything else to wrap around it on the left. Here, we've floated the alpaca picture to the right, so the text flows around the picture.

None: this is the default, but it's sometimes useful to be able to explicitly tell a box, no, don't float.

Inherit: if you do want a box to inherit the float value of its container, just say so explicitly by setting float to inherit.

In the Alpaca Repo site, we've defined two classes, .floatRight and .floatLeft. We can apply these classes to move elements to the right or left as needed.

```
.floatRight {
    float: right;
    margin-left: .8em;
}

.floatLeft {
    float: left;
    margin-right: .8em;
}
```

choose your sizing

CSS sizes come in two flavors: relative and absolute. Relative sizes are those that are defined in terms of their relationship to some element on the page, while absolute sizes are, well, absolute; they are fixed to a particular size.

Overall, the W3C (the organization that sets Web standards) strongly recommends that you use relative sizes on your pages instead of absolute, unless you are absolutely certain of the dimensions of the display device (and that's darned rare for a Web page).

Note that points and pixels are not the same thing at all! While Macs started out with 1pt = 1px, things have changed since the days of the 9" black-and-white screen. And on PCs, points and pixels have never been equivalent.

Relative Sizes

Unit	Definition
em	The width of the letter M in the chosen font
ex	The height of the letter x in the chosen font
px	Pixels

Absolute Sizes

Unit	Definition
pt	Point size, where 1 pt = 1/72 of an inch
in	Inches
mm	Millimeters
cm	Centimeters
pc	Picas, where 1 pc = 1/6 of an inch

create the xhtml

Enough with the theory; now it's time to start building the page. The Alpaca Repo site uses a pretty standard layout: header, sidebar that contains the navigation bar, a main content area, and a footer.

The unit we are primarily using on the site is ems, because we want the site to automatically and properly resize if the user bumps up (or reduces) the text size in their browser.

We've decided that the site will begin with six pages, which will be reflected in the navigation bar: index.html, services.html, faq.html, testimonials.html, about.html, and contact.html.

In your text editor, create an XHTML page, with the usual elements: < head >, < title >, and < body >. Fill in the title. We'll need five divs, which we will give ids to: an overall container that goes inside the < body > tag; a header; a sidebar; the mainContent; and the footer.

The initial XHTML looks like this:

```
<!DOCTYPE html PUBLIC "-//W3C//DTD XHTML 1.0 Transitional//EN"
"http://www.w3.org/TR/xhtml1/DTD/xhtml1-transitional.dtd">
<html xmlns="http://www.w3.org/1999/xhtml">
<head>
    <meta http-equiv="Content-Type" content="text/html;
        charset=UTF-8" />
    <title>Welcome to Alpaca Repo</title>
    <link rel="stylesheet" href="styles.css" type="text/css" />
</head>
<body>
    <div id="container">
        <div id="header">
        </div> <!-- end #header -->
        <div id="sidebar">
        </div> <!-- end #sidebar -->
```


(continued on next page)

create the xhtml (cont.)

(continued from previous page)

```
    <div id="mainContent">
    </div> <!-- end #mainContent -->
    <div id="footer">
    </div>  <!-- end #footer -->
  </div>  <!-- end #container -->
</body>
</html>
```

Notice that the <link> tag in the <head> points to the external stylesheet that we'll create in the next section, called styles.css. Now we'll add some content inside the divs. First, let's add the entries in the navigation bar. Inside the sidebar div, add an unordered list with links to the pages that we'll create. The result looks like this:

```
<div id="sidebar">
    <ul>
        <li><a href="index.html">Home</a></li>
        <li><a href="services.html">Services</a></li>
        <li><a href="faq.html">FAQ</a></li>
        <li><a href="testimonials.html">Testimonials</a></li>
        <li><a href="about.html">About Alpacas</a></li>
        <li><a href="contact.html">Contact Us</a></li>
    </ul>
</div>  <!-- end #sidebar -->
```

In the header div, add the image that is inside the header, like so (of course, your path and image name may be different):

```
<div id="header">
    <img src="images/header.jpg" width="800" height="110"
alt="header" />
</div> <!-- end #header -->
```

Now add some text inside the footer div:

```
<div id="footer">
    <p>Copyright &copy; 2009 Alpaca Repo. All rights reserved.</p>
</div> <!-- end #footer -->
```

Finally, add some text in the mainContent div. We included a couple of headings and some filler text:

```
<div id="mainContent">
    <h2>When They Don't Pay, We Tow 'Em Away</h2>
    <p>Lorem ipsum dolor sit amet, consectetuer adipiscing elit.
Praesent aliquam,  justo convallis luctus rutrum, erat nulla
fermentum diam, at nonummy quam  ante ac quam. Maecenas urna
purus, fermentum id, molestie in, commodo  porttitor, felis.</p>
    <h2>H2 level heading </h2>
    <p>Lorem ipsum dolor sit amet, consectetuer adipiscing elit.
Praesent aliquam,  justo convallis luctus rutrum, erat nulla
fermentum diam, at nonummy quam  ante ac quam.</p>
</div> <!-- end #mainContent -->
```

layout and positioning

create the xhtml (cont.)

The end result is this XHTML:

```
<!DOCTYPE html PUBLIC "-//W3C//DTD XHTML 1.0 Transitional//EN"
"http://www.w3.org/TR/xhtml1/DTD/xhtml1-transitional.dtd">
<html xmlns="http://www.w3.org/1999/xhtml">
<head>
    <meta http-equiv="Content-Type" content="text/html;
        charset=UTF-8" />
    <title>Welcome to Alpaca Repo</title>
    <link rel="stylesheet" href="styles.css" type="text/css" />
</head>
<body>
    <div id="container">
        <div id="header">
            <img src="images/header.jpg" width="800" height="110"
                alt="header" />
        </div>  <!-- end #header -->
        <div id="sidebar">
            <ul>
                <li><a href="index.html">Home</a></li>
                <li><a href="services.html">Services</a></li>
                <li><a href="faq.html">FAQ</a></li>
                <li><a href="testimonials.html">Testimonials</a></li>
                <li><a href="about.html">About Alpacas</a></li>
                <li><a href="contact.html">Contact Us</a></li>
            </ul>
        </div>  <!-- end #sidebar -->
        <div id="mainContent">
            <h2>When They Don't Pay, We Tow 'Em Away</h2>
            <p>Lorem ipsum dolor sit amet, consectetuer adipiscing
elit. Praesent aliquam, justo convallis luctus rutrum, erat
nulla fermentum diam, at nonummy quam ante ac quam. Maecenas
urna purus, fermentum id, molestie in, commodo porttitor,
felis.</p>
```

(continued on next page)

(continued from previous page)

```
        <h2>H2 level heading </h2>
        <p>Lorem ipsum dolor sit amet, consectetuer adipiscing
elit. Praesent aliquam,  justo convallis luctus rutrum, erat
nulla fermentum diam, at nonummy quam  ante ac quam.</p>
    </div> <!-- end #mainContent -->
    <div id="footer">
        <p>Copyright &copy; 2009 Alpaca Repo. All rights
reserved.</p>
    </div> <!-- end #footer -->
  </div> <!-- end #container -->
</body>
</html>
```

That does it for the XHTML for now.

style the divs

The XHTML from the last section creates a pretty dull-looking page, with everything flowing down the page and no added style.

Time to add the CSS rules that will turn our boring XHTML page into something with a bit more snap to it. We'll do that by creating a CSS stylesheet, and adding rules for each of the five divs.

Begin in your text editor by creating a new blank stylesheet. Save it as styles.css.

First, let's style the container div, which surrounds the rest of the layout. Enter this text:

```
#container {
    width: 80%;
    background-color: #EBEBEB;
    margin: 0 auto;
    padding: 0;
    text-align: left;
}
```

There is only one element on the page named container, so we are setting its rule as an id by naming it #container. We're setting the width to be 80%, so that it takes up that percentage of the page. The background-color is a light gray (for reasons we'll get to later). For margin, when you have two values, the first, which in this case is 0, applies to the top and bottom of the box; auto applies to the right and left sides of the box and centers the container on the page. The padding has one value of 0, which applies to all four sides of the box. And finally, we set the text-align to left.

Next, we create the #header id, with this text:

```
#header {
    background-color: #91A43D;
    text-align: center;
    margin: 0;
    padding: 0;
}
```

Header background-color   Header image

The main color in the Alpaca Repo header picture is green, so we set background-color to a nice medium green. This color will appear behind the header image if the user resizes the browser window wider than the image.

Finally, we set the header's margin and padding to zero.

style the divs (cont.)

The next id we'll create is #sidebar. We're going to set it to float to the left, and we'll make it about 12 characters wide (or 12 ems).

```
#sidebar {
    float: left;
    width: 12em;
}
```

Now comes the #mainContent id.

```
#mainContent {
    background-color: #FFFFFF;
    margin-left: 12em;
    padding: 10px 20px 0 1em;
}
```

The mainContent column does not float. The background-color gets set to white. The mainContent column goes to the right of the sidebar, so we give it a margin-left of 12 ems, the same width as the sidebar. For padding, we provide 10 pixels at the top (so the content doesn't butt right up against the header), 20 pixels on the right, 0 pixels at the bottom, and 1 em at the left.

It's fine to mix size values to a certain extent, although you should keep all your text in relative sizes. Just because you use em in one place doesn't mean that you have to use it everywhere. Here, we've used pixels in places where we want to be offset a certain distance from things that are measured in pixels (such as the header graphic) and ems in places where we want to be offset a certain distance from things that are measured in ems (such as the sidebar).

The last div we're styling is #footer. But here, we're not styling the footer itself, but rather, all the paragraphs inside the footer. To do that, we set the selector (remember, that's the part of the rule that defines what the rest of the rule will apply to) to be the div's id followed by a space and the tag we want to style, as shown here:

```
#footer p {
    margin: 0;
    padding: 10px 0;
    background-color: #DDDDDD;
    text-align: center;
    font-size: .8em;
}
```

So, this rule applies to everything inside the <p> tags, so long as those <p> tags are inside the #footer div. By now, you can see that we're setting the margin to 0, and the top and bottom padding to 10 pixels, with no right and left padding. The background-color gets set to a medium gray. We also align the text in the div to center alignment, and set its font-size to .8em, so that it is 80% of the size of the body font.

Things are looking pretty good, but there's a potential problem that we'll solve in the next section.

create faux columns

After styling and positioning the divs, the layout is beginning to look the way we want it to. The problems we alluded to in the last section are twofold. First, on the different pages that we have in the site, we don't know whether sidebar or mainContent will contain the most content. Second, we want both divs to have a background color going all the way down the page, and instead, they stop when the content in that block element stops.

The solution is to create what are called faux columns, which will fake a layout so that it appears to have columns that are the same length. Here's how:

```
#sidebar {
    float: left;
    width: 12em;
}
```

You might have noticed that we never gave the sidebar div a background color—that's because if we set sidebar's background color, it wouldn't always show the color for the entire height of sidebar, but only for that part where there was some text content. The solution is in the container rule.

```
#container {
    width: 80%;
    background-color: #EBEBEB;
    margin: 0 auto;
    padding: 0;
    text-align: left;
}
```

Recall how we skipped explaining why the background color for container was set? Instead of putting the background color on sidebar, we put the sidebar background color on container. That way, once we force sidebar to appear to have the height we want, and so long as we don't give it a background color of its own, the color behind it (that is, container's background color) will just show through.

As a result of this, we have to make sure that header, footer, and mainContent also have their background colors set, which we've already done.

Because we floated sidebar, we need to make sure that mainContent (the area that wraps around sidebar) comes to a complete end before footer starts—otherwise, footer will also wrap around sidebar any time that mainContent is shorter than sidebar. We do that by adding a new class called .clearfloat.

```
.clearfloat {
    clear: both;
    height: 0;
    font-size: 1px;
}
```

And finally, we add this line to mainContent, just before the final <div>.

```
<br class="clearfloat" />
```

Together, these force everything following to display after any previously floated element (whether floated either to the left or right). In this case, footer will now always be after both sidebar and mainContent. The height and font-size are set to 0 and 1px (respectively) to make the <br> take up as little vertical height as possible.

extra bits

block vs inline tags p. 16

- In the spirit of keeping your containers to a minimum, later in the chapter, notice that there are no divs or spans inside the #mainContent or #sidebar divs.

the box model p. 17

- Colors can be set using any of these methods:

Color name	A color name: red
rgb(x,x,x)	An RGB value: rgb(255,0,0)
rgb(x%, x%, x%)	An RGB percentage value: rgb(100%,0%,0%)
#RRGGBB	A 6-digit hex number: #FF0000
#RGB	A 3-digit hex number: #F00

- Valid CSS color names are:

aqua	#00FFFF	rgb(0,255,255)
black	#000000	rgb(0,0,0)
blue	#0000FF	rgb(0,0,255)
fuchsia	#FF00FF	rgb(255,0,255)
gray	#808080	rgb(128,128,128)
green	#008000	rgb(0,128,0)
lime	#00FF00	rgb(0,255,0)
maroon	#800000	rgb(128,0,0)
navy	#000080	rgb(0,0,128)
olive	#808000	rgb(128,128,0)
purple	#800080	rgb(128,0,128)
red	#FF0000	rgb(255,0,0)
silver	#C0C0C0	rgb(192,192,192)
teal	#008080	rgb(0,128,128)
white	#FFFFFF	rgb(255,255,255)
yellow	#FFFF00	rgb(255,255,0)

- You can see a complete list of colors supported by major browsers at http://www.dori.com/css/colors.html.

- You can see the border styles displayed at http://www.dori.com/css/borders.html.

positioning boxes p. 19

- Another kind of positioning, inherit, is used when you want a box to automatically inherit the properties of its parent (that is, its container). Wherever that box happens to be, it just takes on the positioning rules based on its container.

create the xhtml p. 23

- When we created the divs, we also added XHTML comments after each div's closing tag, to help you keep track of which div you are looking at. It's a good idea to do this in your own pages, too.

style the divs p. 28

- We're showing the CSS rules in the vertical form, to make them easier to understand. But remember that you can write them more compactly, as we discussed in Chapter 1.

3. styling text

The main message of most of your Web sites will be conveyed by the site's text. When you add text, you need to deal with two different aspects of the text: its structure and its presentation. The structure, implemented with XHTML, includes things like paragraphs, headings, lists, and the like; presentation (applied using CSS) is how the text looks, including things like the font, font size, text color, and so on.

Using CSS styles, your site doesn't just look good—you get other benefits as well. Because the CSS stylesheet is separate from the XHTML, it's easy to make changes in your site's look simply by modifying the CSS rules in the stylesheet.

In this chapter, we'll focus on creating and applying CSS rules for your site's text.

understand css fonts

To style text with CSS, you need to know that it's a bit different from styling text in say, a word processor, where you simply select some text and choose a font and font styles from a menu. With CSS, you create rules, and these rules can style anything defined by an XHTML tag, class, or id.

A CSS rule consists of a selector followed by declarations, as we've seen in past chapters. Declarations contain properties, which, in turn, have values. So, for example, if we wanted to style all < h2 > tags in the document with a serif font, bold, and colored gray, we could write this rule:

```
h2 {
    font-family: Georgia, "Times New Roman", Times, serif;
    color: gray;
    font-weight: bold;
}
```

We can see immediately that there's something unusual going on here, from the standpoint of a designer that comes from the print world. In that world, you set the type using the font family you want, and that's the end of it. But that approach doesn't work on the Web, because the installed fonts are different on the myriad of computer and mobile platforms that can browse the Web. Macs don't come with the same fonts as Windows or Linux machines, and mobile devices like the BlackBerry or iPhone add even more possible fonts to the mix. That's why with CSS, instead of specifying a font, you use the font-family property to provide a list of fonts the Web browser should look for, in the order that it should try them in, separated by commas. So because you don't have exact control over the typeface, it follows that you don't have exact control over how the page will look for all readers, either. Just relax and get used to it.

Font Properties

This table shows the properties and associated values that you can use to style fonts.

Property	Value
font	< font-style >
	< font-variant >
	< font-weight >
	< font-size > /
	< line-height >
	< font-family >
	caption
	icon
	menu
	message-box
	small-caption
	status-bar
font-family	< family-name >
	cursive
	fantasy
	monospace
	sans-serif
	serif
font-size	< absolute-size >
	(xx-small–xx-large)
	< relative-size >
	(smaller–larger)
	< length >
	< percentage >
font-style	normal
	italic
	oblique
font-variant	normal
	small-caps
font-weight	normal
	bold
	bolder
	lighter
	100 – 900

Text Properties

Text properties add additional options for the appearance of text. This table shows text properties and values.

Property	Value
letter-spacing	normal
	< length >
text-align	left
	right
	center
	justify
text-decoration	none
	underline
	overline
	line-through
	blink
text-indent	< length >
	< percentage >
text-transform	capitalize
	uppercase
	lowercase
	none
white-space	normal
	pre
	nowrap
	pre-wrap
	pre-line
word-spacing	normal
	< length >

understand css fonts ^(cont.)

As a general approach, choose fonts using this rule:

font-family: ideal, alternative, common, generic

Here are some recommendations for different sorts of font groups:

Sans-serif: font-family: Arial, Helmet, Freesans, sans-serif;

Serif: font-family: Cambria, "Times New Roman", "Nimbus Roman No9 L", Freeserif, Times, serif;

Monospaced: font-family: "Courier New", Courier, Freemono, "Nimbus Mono L", monospace;

Notice how when you have a font name that contains a space, you need to put quotes (") around the name. See the extra bits for more information about the generic fonts.

style text

On the Alpaca Repo site, we're going to style most of the text with a sans-serif font, starting with Verdana. The easiest way to do that is to restyle the < body > tag. By restyling body, we change the look of all of the text in the document, and we don't have to add any extra classes or ids at this time.

```
body {
    font-family: Verdana, Geneva, "Bitstream Vera Sans",
                 "DejaVu Sans", sans-serif;
    background-color: #666666;
    color: #000000;
    margin: 0;
    padding: 0;
    text-align: center;
}
```

This rule first sets the font-family to a series of sans-serif fonts. The background-color property is set to a dark gray, which you can see on the left and right sides of the columns in the picture below. The color property sets the text to black. Margin and padding are both set to zero. And finally, we set text-align to center the container div on the page.

style text (cont.)

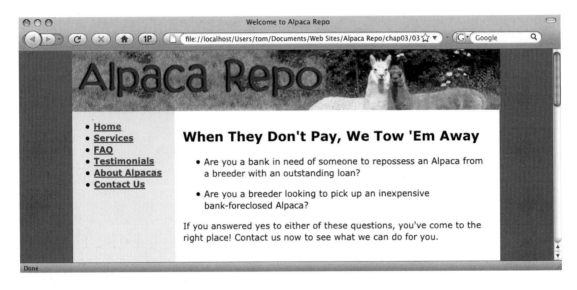

While we are styling text, let's add some properties to the #sidebar id.

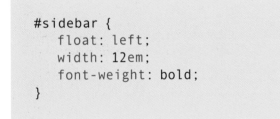

```
#sidebar {
    float: left;
    width: 12em;
    font-weight: bold;
}
```

You can see in the picture that the links in the sidebar are bold. We are adding the bold property now as a little prep work for when we turn the links into a navigation menu in Chapter 5.

style headings

The page is coming along, but we're not so happy with the look of the headings. Let's change the look of all heading tags by turning them into a serif font. And because we want all the sizes of headings to appear in this font, let's change all of them at once.

```
h1, h2, h3, h4, h5, h6 {
    font-family: Cambria, "Palatino Linotype", "Book
                 Antiqua", "URW Palladio L", serif;
}
```

As we mentioned previously, a selector can apply to multiple XHTML tags by simply separating the tags with commas. The result of the rule addition appears at the top of the mainContent div, and makes the page a bit more interesting and easier to read.

Styled heading

extra bits

understand css fonts p. 38

- When the user sees a Web page, if none of the font options listed in font-family are available, browsers will fall back to the generic font. The generic fonts may be displayed as one of many different fonts, depending on which fonts are installed on the computer and the browser being used. Here are some commonly found fonts that we've seen used for each of the generic font names:

  Serif: Times New Roman, Times

  Sans-serif: Helvetica, Arial, Tahoma

  Cursive: Comic Sans MS, Apple Chancery

  Monospace: Courier New, Courier

  Fantasy: Can be anything at all, depending on the platform and browser.

- The user can set their own font preferences for generic fonts in some browsers. For example, Safari and Internet Explorer 7 let you pick two fonts, a "standard" font and a monospace font. Firefox lets you pick a proportional sans-serif font, a proportional serif font, a monospace font, and whether the default font is sans-serif or serif.

- It's generally a better idea to use sans-serif fonts on the Web, especially for paragraph text. The Web is displayed on screens that are much lower resolution than print, so the extra details of serif type can get lost, particularly at smaller sizes.

styling text

style text p. 41

- If you're used to word processors or page layout programs, you may think that bold and italic are applied in the same property, but that's not the case with CSS. The former is a value for font-weight, and the latter is a value for font-style.

- The text properties can add some interesting options to your text styling. For example, by adding

  text-decoration:underline overline;

  to the heading rule that we defined, you can set off the text even more.

  ### When They Don't Pay, We Tow 'Em Away

  - Are you a bank in need of someone to repossess an a breeder with an outstanding loan?

- If you're a designer looking to control the leading of your type, you can do it using the line-height property. Similarly, you can use the letter-spacing and word-spacing properties for more control over the kerning and tracking, respectively, of text. Keep in mind, though, that browser support for these last two properties is uneven, at best.

- Instead of using the individual properties for (for example) font-style, font-size, and font-weight, you can use font as a shorthand property by itself to combine them all. For example:

  font: italic bold 1.2em "andale mono";

  When you use the font property, it must contain at least a font-size and a font-family, in that order. If you use font-style, or font-weight, put them before the other two properties.

- The italic and oblique values for font-style do the same thing. Sorry, typographers!

4. work with images

Images convey an important amount of the message of your Web site. Indeed, for some sites, images tell virtually the entire story of the site. For our Alpaca Repo site, we're using images sparingly, to illustrate the text, rather than making images the star of the show.

In this chapter, we'll first go into a little detail about preparing images for the Web. Then we'll show you how you use CSS to position images on your Web pages, as with the photo and caption floated to the right on the page shown below. And finally, we'll go through the rules we created to place the images on our pages.

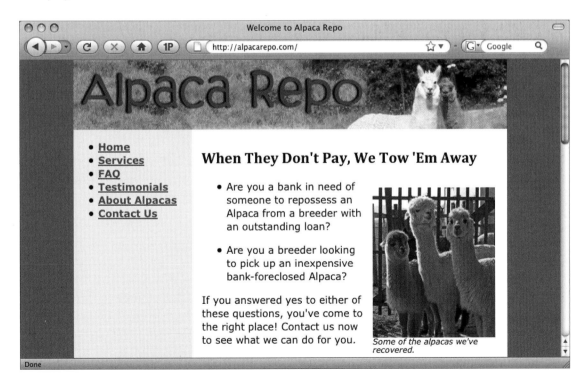

prepare images

When you're working on your sites, you'll need to have a good image editing program available to prepare your images for the Web. That preparation will take three steps:

1 Resampling the image so that it is at the proper resolution for the Web.

2 Resizing or cropping the image so it is the right size on your page.

3 Saving the image in one of the three Web image formats.

The first step, resampling, is important, because Web graphics are inherently low-resolution, being designed to be viewed on-screen. There's no need to have photos on your site be more than the resolution of the screen, which will be between 72 and 96 dpi (dots per inch). The extra resolution is wasted, and higher-resolution photos have larger file sizes, which will make your Web page load more slowly. So if you have photos taken by a digital camera, which is usally much higher resolution, you should reduce the resolution with your graphics editor.

Reducing the resolution will usually change the width and height of the picture, depending on your image editor. Many editors allow you to see how resolution changes affect image size.

In this Photoshop dialog, changing the resolution for a digital photograph from its native 180 pixels/inch to 72 pixels/inch proportionally changes its width and height, too.

work with images

Once you have the proper resolution, you should crop or resize the image to show only the important part of the image. Here, we've selected the area we want with the crop tool. After reducing the resolution and cropping, the image is the size that we want.

Crop area

Finally, save the image in one of the three Web graphics formats: JPEG, PNG, or GIF. See the extra bits for more details on these formats.

float images

To place an image on a page, you simply insert the `<img>` tag in the flow of the page. This however, may not get you the result you want, as the image appears with text above and below it.

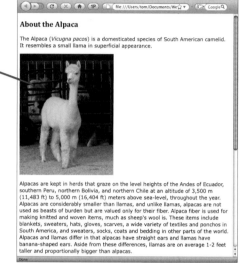

To get the text to wrap around the image, you need to float the image to the right or to the left. If you float a box element (let's call it theAlpaca) to the right, anything outside theAlpaca will wrap around to its left.

`#theAlpaca {float: right;}`

If you instead float it to the left, anything outside theAlpaca will wrap around to its right.

`#theAlpaca {float: left;}`

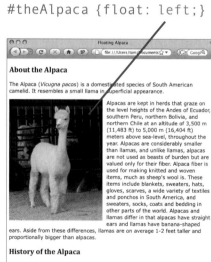

Let's say that you had a heading in the text as well.

But we don't want that heading to be on the side of the alpaca, as it's important. Additionally, when the headline is next to the alpaca, it appears that it's about the alpaca—but it's not.

To fix that, we want it to always be on a line by itself, and to do that, we need to clear the float.

```
#theAlpaca {float: right;}
h1 {clear: right;}
```

That pushes the heading down below the image.

That's what you need to know about floating and clearing box elements. You can do this for any box element, not just images. You can float divs, paragraphs, whatever.

place images

Now let's put the theory into practice for the photos on the Alpaca Repo site. First, in the styles.css file, we'll need to create three new classes to handle photos: floatRight, floatLeft, and photo.

The photo class sets up the styling for the photo and its caption that we use on the front page of the site.

```
.photo {
    width: 200px;
    font-size: .8em;
    font-style: italic;
    line-height: 1em;
}
```

Let's also look at the XHTML for the image, which is in the index.html file:

```
<p class="photo floatRight"><img src="images/3alpacas.jpg"
width="200" height="237" alt="alpacas" />Some of the alpacas
we've recovered.</p>
```

In this XHTML, you can see that we've put the image inside a paragraph, which is a block element. We've applied two class attributes to the paragraph: photo and floatRight, each of which has a rule inside styles.css. Let's explain what those rules do.

The photo class makes this paragraph block have a width of 200 pixels—the same width as the image. Because the paragraph is set to be the same width as the image, the caption, which is inside the paragraph tags, goes under the image without any need for a break or second paragraph. The photo class also sets the text in the paragraph to be italic, and sets the font size and line height, so the caption has the style of our choice.

work with images

The floatLeft and floatRight classes just push the block to either the left or the right, with other text wrapping around it. There's also a margin here to keep a little offset to make the picture pop. Because the margin is applied to the entire paragraph, the caption does not get pushed away by the margin.

```
.floatRight {
    float: right;
    margin-left: .8em;
}

.floatLeft {
    float: left;
    margin-right: .8em;
}
```

Next, in the site's index.html file, there's a line that says

```
<br clear="right" />
```

In this particular case, we had floated the photo to the right, so we clear it by giving clear a value of right. That bit of markup forces the following paragraphs to go below the right-floated photo instead of wrapping around it.

In case we want to clear all of our floats, we've also created a class that does that, which we've cleverly called clearfloat.

```
.clearfloat {
    clear: both;
    height: 0;
    font-size: 1px;
}
```

See that the clear property has the value of both? That means that any element with clearfloat applied to it clears all elements floated to either the left or right.

work with images   **53**

place images (cont.)

We don't want to use the clearfloat class after the images inside #mainContent, though, because it would clear the sidebar as well (remember that we floated the sidebar in Chapter 2, and we don't want to force everything following to go after the sidebar ends).

If index.html used floatLeft for the photo instead of floatRight, that line above would instead have to be

```
<br clear="left" />
```

However, then we'd have the same possible problem—clearing the left-floated item would also clear the sidebar, forcing the following paragraphs way down the page. That isn't a problem when your sidebar is short (as ours is here), but it's something to keep in mind.

One more thing that relates to images, then we're done with this page. We've added a property to the header rule we created back in Chapter 2, so that it looks like this:

```
#header {
    background-color: #91A43D;
    text-align: center;
    margin: 0;
    padding: 0;
    overflow: hidden;
}
```

The property that we added, overflow: hidden; is what performs the cool shrinking effect when we make any page narrow. All it does is tell the browser that if there isn't enough room to display the entire header image, don't worry about it. Just hide whatever doesn't fit. This allows us to have a wide header image that shows just what we want it to show, but it doesn't force the window to be a particular width.

add background images

We're not using them on the Alpaca Repo site, but it's not uncommon to want to use background images on your page, so we're covering them here. A background image can be any graphic, but they are usually small images that can tile seamlessly when they are repeated. You can use CSS to tile them over the whole page (the default) or tile the image in the horizontal (x) direction or the vertical (y) direction. Of course, you don't have to use a background image on just the < body > tag so that it covers the whole page; you can add a background image to any div or other block element.

To add a background image, just add this property to a block element:

```
background-image: url(images/background.jpg);
```

Notice that there are no quotes around the URL.
The image we're using for this example looks like this:

By default, the image will tile across and down the page, as shown here. If you want to set that to happen explicitly, though, just say:

```
background-repeat: repeat;
```

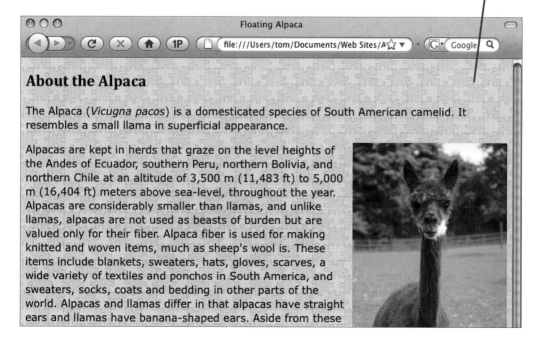

About the Alpaca

The Alpaca (*Vicugna pacos*) is a domesticated species of South American camelid. It resembles a small llama in superficial appearance.

Alpacas are kept in herds that graze on the level heights of the Andes of Ecuador, southern Peru, northern Bolivia, and northern Chile at an altitude of 3,500 m (11,483 ft) to 5,000 m (16,404 ft) meters above sea-level, throughout the year. Alpacas are considerably smaller than llamas, and unlike llamas, alpacas are not used as beasts of burden but are valued only for their fiber. Alpaca fiber is used for making knitted and woven items, much as sheep's wool is. These items include blankets, sweaters, hats, gloves, scarves, a wide variety of textiles and ponchos in South America, and sweaters, socks, coats and bedding in other parts of the world. Alpacas and llamas differ in that alpacas have straight ears and llamas have banana-shaped ears. Aside from these

background images (cont.)

To control the horizontal and vertical tiling of the image, use one of these properties:

```
background-repeat: repeat-x;
background-repeat: repeat-y;
```

The latter looks like this:

About the Alpaca

The Alpaca (*Vicugna pacos*) is a dom‹
resembles a small llama in superficial

Alpacas are kept in herds that graze ‹
the Andes of Ecuador, southern Peru,
northern Chile at an altitude of 3,500
m (16,404 ft) meters above sea-leve‹
Alpacas are considerably smaller thar
llamas, alpacas are not used as beas‹
valued only for their fiber. Alpaca fibe
knitted and woven items, much as sh

extra bits

prepare images p. 48

- There are three main still (as opposed to moving) image formats used on the Web: GIF, JPEG, and PNG. GIF is a lower-resolution image format that can only contain up to 256 colors. GIFs are usually used for line drawings, flat cartoons, logos and other images that don't need thousands or millions of colors (for example, a photograph). JPEG is the most common image format for photographs, and it can handle millions of colors. The JPEG format is "lossy," which means it uses compression to reduce file size. The look of the image depends on the amount of compression used to record it. The higher the compression, the more noticeable the image degradation. But most of the time you can use a moderate level of compression, reduce the file size significantly, and see little visual effect. A PNG file supports millions of colors, and is suitable for either simple images or photographs. Both PNG and GIF support transparency, which means that you can set one or more colors in the file to be either the same as the background color of the page (GIF) or to have no color at all (PNG). PNG is a newer and more capable format, and we generally recommend that you use it instead of GIF when preparing your Web images.

- Almost any image editing program will work just fine to prepare graphics for the Web. The traditional big gun is Adobe Photoshop, but you can get by with much cheaper and simpler programs. On the Mac, our inexpensive favorites include Graphic Converter (www.lemkesoft.com), or if you need more power, Pixelmator (www.pixelmator.com). On Windows, we like two free programs: Picasa (picasa.google.com) or GIMP (www.gimp.org), which is also available for Mac.

place images p. 52

- Other values for overflow are: auto, which shows scrollbars when necessary; scroll, which shows scrollbars (both horizontal and vertical) whether they're needed or not; and visible, the default.

- If your site uses images as links (the Alpaca Repo site doesn't, but it's common), you might be wondering how you can eliminate the blue border that some browsers show around the image that indicates it is a link. Once again, a simple line of CSS to the rescue! Just add this line to your stylesheet:

  `a img {border-width: 0;}`

  That is, set the border width to zero for all images that are inside an `<a>` tag.

extra bits

add background images p. 55

- There are a number of properties for background images and colors, as shown in this table.

Color and Background Properties

Property	Value
background	< background-color > < background-image > < background-repeat > < background-attachment > < background-position >
background-attachment	scroll fixed
background-color	< color > transparent
background-image	< url > none
background-position	< percentage > < length > top center bottom left right
background-repeat	repeat repeat-x repeat-y no-repeat
color	< color >

work with images

5. make menus

Every site needs a way for your visitors to navigate around it. Usually, that means a menu of one sort or another. There are different ways to create menus on Web sites, and you've probably seen many of them, some using JavaScript, fancier ones using Ajax, and even ones using Flash.

In this chapter, we're going to discover how to create good-looking menus using nothing more than an XHTML unordered list, styled with CSS.

On the Alpaca Repo site, we previously created an unordered list with the site's navigation, and put it in the sidebar. Each item in the list is a link to another page. By adding rules to our CSS stylesheet, we can change the look of the list so that it looks like a menubar, and even add rollover effects.

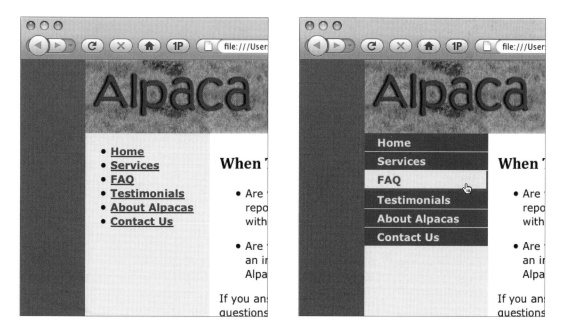

style the sidebar

The sidebar div is where we've put the site navigation. We start with that div, which is wrapped around an XHTML unordered list (<ul>). Within the <ul>, each list item is enclosed in a <li> tag. The text of each list item is a link, so each is wrapped in an <a> tag. Here's what this XHTML looks like:

```
<div id="sidebar">
    <ul>
        <li><a href="index.html">Home</a></li>
        <li><a href="services.html">Services</a></li>
        <li><a href="faq.html">FAQ</a></li>
        <li><a href="testimonials.html">Testimonials</a></li>
        <li><a href="about.html">About Alpacas</a></li>
        <li><a href="contact.html">Contact Us</a></li>
    </ul>
</div> <!-- end #sidebar -->
```

Unordered lists, in general, look like the list on the site's home page, shown on the opening page of this chapter. You have bullets, you have text, and you automatically get some space around the <ul> block.

In the styles.css file, add the following rule:

```
#sidebar ul {
    margin: 0;
    padding: 0;
    list-style-type: none;
}
```

This rule targets only the ul element inside the sidebar. The benefit of this is that it means that any bulleted lists inside other divs (such as mainContent) aren't affected by the rule. Setting the list-style-type to none gets rid of the automatic bullets from the list. See the extra bits for more CSS list options. Along with getting rid of the bullet, we also want to get rid of the space around the ul—that's the reason we set padding and margin to 0. The result gives us a list that is no longer bulleted, and it's snug against the header and the left side of the sidebar.

create the buttons

To change the appearance of the links in the list to look like buttons, we'll add another rule to the styles.css file.

```
#sidebar a {
    display: block;
    padding: 3px 3px 5px 30px;
    background-color: #336666;
    color: #EBEBEB;
    border-bottom: 1px #EBEBEB solid;
    text-decoration: none;
}
```

This rule applies to all the < a > tags inside the sidebar div. The display: block rule is where the magic happens. Back in Chapter 1, we said that every element was either block or inline. Of course, a elements, which create links, are inline—right? But here we tell the browser we want the links to be block elements instead. That's how we start to get our button appearance.

Next, we put some padding around our nacent button. We're using 3 pixels for the top and right, 5 pixels for the bottom, and 30 pixels for the left side, to push the text of the links away from the edge of the sidebar. Now we've got nice big button areas we can click.

The background-color property is the actual color of the button itself. We gave it a nice green that we picked out of the header image.

The color property is the color of the text inside the buttons. We picked the same gray here as is used on the rest of the sidebar. That makes the text match the sidebar, and look consistent overall.

By adding the border-bottom property, we create a single pixel bottom border that's the same color as the rest of the sidebar (and the text). This makes it appear as if the buttons don't butt up against each other, so it's easier to see which is which.

Notice that the 5 pixel padding and the 1 pixel bottom border add up to a total of 6 pixels. This will matter later in this chapter when we add rollover effects.

And finally, we set text-decoration to none. That tells the links to not be underlined, so again, they look more like buttons.

The end result of this rule is a list that has been transformed into a set of buttons.

add rollover effects

Now that we've created the buttons, we want to give them a rollover effect, so that when the user hovers the cursor over a button the appearance of the button changes, giving feedback to the user.

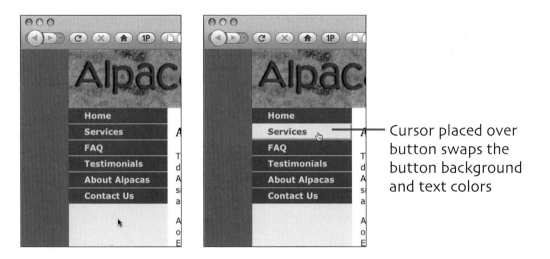

Cursor placed over button swaps the button background and text colors

To the browser, the user interacting with the page by pointing or clicking on an element on the page triggers what is called an event. As a Web page creator, if you want the page to react to the user's events, you have a variety of tools at your disposal, including JavaScript and CSS. Rather than learn JavaScript to do a simple rollover, however, let's just use CSS. To do that, we'll introduce a new concept: the pseudo-class. Pseudo-classes apply rules when certain events occur, and pseudo-classes are always applied to other elements.

That is, you have an element of some kind, and then you apply one of the pseudo-classes listed below. The syntax is element, colon, pseudo-class. For instance, a link can have the pseudo-class visited applied to it, which would be written as: a:visited { color: #FF00FF; }. That would make any previously visited links be kind of purplish.

Pseudo-classes are commonly used with a tags, which create links, and that's how we'll use them here. There are four pseudo-classes for the a tag.

Pseudo-Classes

Selector	What it applies to
:link	Applies to unvisited links, i.e., it will not apply to all links, just those that the user hasn't yet been to.
:visited	Applies to links that have been visited.
:hover	Applies to the link that is currently being pointed at.
:active	Applies to the link that is being clicked.

Since each button in the Alpaca Repo sidebar is a link, we'll want to add one more rule that applies to the a tags. Enter this rule in the styles.css file:

```css
#sidebar a:hover {
    background-color: #EBEBEB;
    color: #336666;
    border-right: 3px #999999 solid;
    border-bottom: 3px #999999 solid;
    padding-bottom: 3px;
}
```

We start this rule by adding the :hover pseudo-class to the a elements in the sidebar, which means that this rule will only take effect when the user is pointing at a link. If you look back at the last rule that we added, you can see that this rule swaps the background-color of the button and the color of the text. In other words, we go from gray on green to green on gray. Next we add 3 pixel wide solid dark gray borders to the right and bottom of the button. Finally we set the padding on the bottom of the button to 3 pixels.

add rollover effects (cont.)

Recall in the last section, we told you to remember that the total of the padding and the bottom border of each button is 6 pixels? Here's why we said to remember that. In this rule, if you add the bottom padding (3 pixels) + the bottom border (3 pixels), you get, again, 6 pixels. That makes the regular version and the hover version of the button the same size. If you don't make sure of that, instead of a nice rollover effect, the button will actually appear to move when the user hovers over it.

So you might be wondering, why reset the right and bottom sides of the button to dark gray at all? If they were not reset, the button would maintain its appearance and you wouldn't have to worry about making sure that the size adds up exactly. The reason is that by resetting those sides, it gives the button a three-dimensional effect that provides a better visual cue for the user that things are changing when the button is being hovered over.

When we move the mouse away from the links, the display automatically goes back to the non-hover version.

The great part about using CSS to create these effects is that if we add a new option to the menu, all that needs to be done is a little XHTML. Just add a link, and it all works via the magic of CSS. No extra CSS, no extra JavaScript, and no graphics to create.

extra bits

style the sidebar p. 60

- Here are the other CSS list options (you can see them in action at www.dori.com/css/lists.html:

List Properties

Property	Value
list-style	< list-style-type >
< list-style-position >
< list-style-image >
list-style-image	< url >
none
list-style-position	inside
outside
list-style-type	disc
circle
square
decimal
decimal-leading-zero
lower-roman
upper-roman
lower-greek
lower-alpha
lower-latin
upper-alpha
upper-latin
armenian
georgian
none

extra bits

create the buttons p. 62

- In the CSS rule, we could have targeted the < a > tag even more specifically, by using any of these:

  #sidebar ul li a

  #sidebar ul a

  #sidebar li a

  But there was no need to get that specific, so we kept it simple. In general, that's a good idea; the simpler you write your rules, the more readable they will be to you and others when they need to be changed down the road.

- We covered text-decoration in Chapter 3, but we didn't say anything about how it is used with links. Many sites these days use these rules:

  a {text-decoration: none; font-weight: bold; }

  This turns off underlining for links and makes the link text bold.

  a:hover {text-decoration: underline; }

  This tells the browser that when the user hovers the mouse over the link text, underline it.

make menus

add rollover effects p. 64

- In this chapter, we're doing simple rollovers with CSS, but there are many rollover and other effects that you might want to do that can only be accomplished using JavaScript. If you want to know more about rollovers and many other features of JavaScript, the essential Web programming language, we are happy to recommend another book we wrote, the best-selling JavaScript and Ajax for the Web: Visual QuickStart Guide, Seventh Edition.

- If the user has a browser that doesn't handle CSS (for whatever reason), they'll still get the ability to click on links; they just won't get the button effect. Instead, it'll look just like an unordered list of links.

- You can use any combination of the link pseudo-classes (in other words you don't have to define all four of them), but if you use more than one, they must be in the order shown in the table. That is, l-v-h-a. Someone came up with a mnemonic of "love-hate" to remember this which works as well as anything.

- The link and visited pseudo-classes apply only to links, but the hover and active pseudo-classes can be applied to anything that you can hover over or activate. For example, you can apply them to form fields or images.

- If the user has a browser that displays CSS but doesn't handle hover (for example, the iPhone) they'll get the nice menu, but not the hover effect.

6. style specific elements

In previous chapters, we've seen how we can select and style elements by XHTML tag name, by class, by id, and by elements that are inside other elements. Those methods of selecting will suffice in many, if not most cases. But sometimes, you need to zero in on particular elements on a page in order to style them. For example, you might want to style alternating rows in a table, as shown on this page. Or you might want to change the first letter in a paragraph to give the effect of a drop cap. Using CSS, you can get as specific as you like about the page elements you want to style.

You may or may not use all of the examples in this chapter in your own sites; we've included them here to teach you more about particular CSS selectors, and how to accomplish particular tasks. We also suggest that you go back and review the "understand the cascade" section of Chapter 1, if you're not clear how the cascade works.

Alpaca fiber

Type	Condition	Color	$/lb.
Huacaya	raw	gray	48
Huacaya	raw	black	32
Huacaya	raw	white	12
Huacaya	raw	fawn/beige	32
Huacaya	raw	brown	24
Suri	washed	gray	72
Suri	washed	black	80
Suri	washed	white	40
Suri	washed	fawn/beige	64
Suri	washed	brown	45

style a table

It's common these days to want to add CSS styles to tables. You can get very fancy with formatting, styling rows, columns, or combinations. You can also add rollover effects to help the user see the information better. In this section, we're going to show you three methods of styling a table. The selectors and techniques we're using aren't limited to tables, however; you can use them throughout your sites, wherever you need to style specific elements.

Alpaca fiber

Type	Condition	Color	$/lb.
Huacaya	raw	gray	48
Huacaya	raw	black	32
Huacaya	raw	white	12
Huacaya	raw	fawn/beige	32
Huacaya	raw	brown	24
Suri	washed	gray	72
Suri	washed	black	80
Suri	washed	white	40
Suri	washed	fawn/beige	64
Suri	washed	brown	45

On the services.html page of the Alpaca Repo site, we've added a table of different kinds of alpaca fiber the site has for sale. For this first example, the table columns have bold headers, with a green bottom border for each cell in the top row. When the user hovers the mouse over a row, the cell background color turns light green, highlighting the items in the row.

There are five rules that apply the styling to the table.

Many of the properties in these rules are familiar from earlier in this book, and to save space, we won't explain them again. The new selectors, new properties, or properties we're using in new ways, will need some explanation. All of these rules target various aspects of the fiberChart id, which is assigned to the table in the services.html page.

In the first rule, border-spacing: 6px; adds 6 pixels of space between the borders of adjacent cells. If you remember the cellspacing attribute in XHTML tables, you'll see that border-spacing is similar, but for CSS. This CSS attribute hasn't been used much until recently, because Internet Explorer (up until IE 8) didn't support it.

style specific elements

```
#fiberChart {
    border-spacing: 6px;
}

#fiberChart td {
    padding: 1px 10px;
}

#fiberChart tr:first-child td {
    font-weight: bold;
    border-bottom: 2px #006600 solid;
}

#fiberChart tr:hover {
    background-color: #BAE8BF;
}

#fiberChart td+td+td+td {
    text-align: right;
}
```

In the third rule, tr:first-child td uses the first-child pseudo-class. As a reminder, in an XHTML table, the tr tag denotes a table row, and td defines a cell in a table. For tr:first-child, read it as "Find the row that is the first child of the parent element, i.e., find the first row of the table"—that is, while there are a number of rows in the table, only the first row is the first tr child of the parent table. For the compound selector tr:first-child td, you should read it as "Any cell in the first row of the table." The rule then goes on to set the font weight and sets a green bottom border for the cells.

Note that we're selecting tr:first-child, not table:first-child. While you might think that we'd want to select the first child of the table, that's not the way :first-child works. Instead, we want to select the first child row in the table, so :first-child is applied to the row itself.

style specific elements

style a table (cont.)

In the fourth rule, we use tr:hover. We introduced the :hover pseudo-class in Chapter 5. Here, we're showing how you can use it with something other than a link. Note that each row changes its background color when the visitor hovers over that row.

In the last rule, the td + td + td + td selector says, "Look for any cells that are the fourth cell in a row," that is, you'll have a match any time you have the fourth cell and on. That is, if this table had five cells across, this would match the last two cells, and so on. The + is the sibling selector, which is all about selecting elements that are adjacent. The compound selectors that we've seen up to this point have all been about something that is inside something else (for example, p img, which selects an image that is inside a paragraph). The sibling selector is all about what elements are next to each other. See the extra bits for more about adjacency. All the rule is doing here is right-aligning the contents of the cells in the right-most column. And that's all there is to styling this table.

But what if you want to add a bit more complexity to the styling? One popular and attractive way to display a table is with zebra-striping, where alternating rows of the table are shown with different background colors.

Alpaca fiber

Type	Condition	Color	$/lb.
Huacaya	raw	gray	48
Huacaya	raw	black	32
Huacaya	raw	white	12
Huacaya	raw	fawn/beige	32
Huacaya	raw	brown	24
Suri	washed	gray	72
Suri	washed	black	80
Suri	washed	white	40
Suri	washed	fawn/beige	64
Suri	washed	brown	45

style specific elements

Here's the CSS used for this version of the table:

```css
#fiberChart {
    border-collapse: collapse;
}

#fiberChart td {
    padding: 10px;
}

#fiberChart td:last-child {
    text-align: right;
}

#fiberChart tr:first-child td {
    font-weight: bold;
    border-bottom: 2px #006600 solid;
}

#fiberChart tr+tr+tr,
#fiberChart tr+tr+tr+tr+tr,
#fiberChart tr+tr+tr+tr+tr+tr+tr,
#fiberChart tr+tr+tr+tr+tr+tr+tr+tr+tr,
#fiberChart tr+tr+tr+tr+tr+tr+tr+tr+tr+tr+tr {
    background-color: #EEEEEE;
    border-bottom: 2px #006600 solid;
}

#fiberChart tr+tr,
#fiberChart tr+tr+tr+tr,
#fiberChart tr+tr+tr+tr+tr+tr,
#fiberChart tr+tr+tr+tr+tr+tr+tr+tr,
#fiberChart tr+tr+tr+tr+tr+tr+tr+tr+tr+tr {
    background-color: #BAE8BF;
    border-bottom-width: 0;
}
```

style a table (cont.)

This targets the fiberChart id, and each rule modifies elements of the table.

In the first rule, the border-collapse property is the more traditional of the CSS ways to style a table. With borders collapsed, you (1) don't get any space between cells, and (2) if you have two borders next to each other (say, every row has both a top and bottom border), they'll collapse into each other. That is, instead of 2px bottom border + 2px top border producing a 4px border, it will be a 2 pixel border.

In the third rule, the td:last-child selector is the more flexible, modern way of doing the same function we performed in the last rule of the previous example (that is, to select the right-most column, and right align its contents). However, note that there is no current or planned IE support for this selector, so the previously shown way to do the job may be safer.

In the fifth and sixth rules, we use the sibling selectors to select the odd and even rows of the table, respectively.

In the fifth rule, we select the third, fifth, seventh, ninth, and eleventh table rows (if the table is shorter, the selector finds no match, and has no effect). Then the rule applies a light gray background color, and a 2 pixel solid green bottom border to the row.

The sixth rule selects the second, fourth, sixth, eighth, and tenth rows and sets the background color of the rows to light green. Setting border-bottom-width to zero on the even rule makes it so that every other row has a border, cutting the table into sections for a nice effect.

If you find this a little confusing, remember what we said about specificity (in understand the cascade) in Chapter 1: when deciding which rule takes precedence, it's all about which is the most specific. If you take the zebra-striping rules individually, the tr+tr, for example, applies to every row from the second on (that is, it applies to row 2 because it's next to row 1, and to row 3 because it's next to row 2, and so on). But tr+tr+tr is more specific than tr+tr, so it applies to rows 3 and up—that is, row 3 is next to 1 and 2; row 4 is next to 2 and 3, and so on, so that rule applies to those. But wait! The tr+tr+tr+tr rule is even more specific, so it overrides the previous rules, applying to rows 4 and up. And so on, and so on, up until the last rule, which applies to the last row.

The third way to format the table produces the same zebra-striping as the method we just used, but it is easier to understand and much more flexible. The drawback is that it uses a selector, nth-child, that is part of the emerging CSS3 standard. That means that it is supported by the latest versions of Safari and Firefox (3.1 and later), but is not supported by any currently existing version of Internet Explorer. So you should use this method only in situations where you know that your users will be using browsers that can support it or when the zebra-striping isn't a major design element.

The look of the table in this example is a little different; we've chosen to put visible borders around all the cells, and put thicker borders after every other row.

Alpaca fiber			
Type	Condition	Color	$/lb.
Huacaya	raw	gray	48
Huacaya	raw	black	32
Huacaya	raw	white	12
Huacaya	raw	fawn/beige	32
Huacaya	raw	brown	24
Suri	washed	gray	72
Suri	washed	black	80
Suri	washed	white	40
Suri	washed	fawn/beige	64
Suri	washed	brown	45

style a table (cont.)

The CSS that produces these effects is much shorter than that in previous examples.

```css
#fiberChart {
    border-collapse: collapse;
    border: 2px #A7A7A7 solid;
}

#fiberChart td {
    padding: 10px;
    border: 1px #A7A7A7 solid;
    background-color: #BAE8BF;
}

#fiberChart tr:nth-child(even) td {
    background-color: #EEEEEE;
    border-bottom: 2px #006600 solid;
}
```

The first rule begins with the border-collapse property, as shown earlier, then adds a 2 pixel solid border around the table itself.

The second rule sets all cells to have padding, a background color, and a 1 pixel border.

The last rule uses nth-child(even), which overrides the second rule for the even-numbered rows. Using this selector, you don't have to jump through the hoops we did in the previous example: nth-child(even) only applies to even-numbered rows, so we can create a blanket rule that applies to the whole table (which will end up applying to only the odd-numbered rows) and then override it for the specific rows we want to target (the even rows), and for just the specific rules that we want to override.

style specific elements

add fancy headings

On our page, we have the title "Alpaca fiber" above the table. The line is styled as a h4 heading. That's fine, but it does look a little dull. Let's jazz it up a little by making it start with a fancy capital letter. This CSS will do the trick.

```css
h4:first-letter {
    font-size: 2em;
    font-family: cursive;
}

h3 + h4 {
    padding: 5px;
    text-align: center;
}
```

And the result looks like this:

Let's deconstruct the CSS. The h4:first-letter selector applies to the first text character inside an h4 heading. The font-size is set to 2em, and the font-family is set to the generic cursive value. This rule makes the headings look larger and more impressive.

The line "Alpaca Fiber for sale" is tagged as an h3 heading. The h3 + h4 selector applies to every h4 that comes directly after an h3—which means it only applies here to the very first h4 on the page, where it centers the heading.

Our services
Alpaca Fiber for sale

*A*lpaca fiber

Type	Condition	Color	$/lb.
Huacaya	raw	gray	48
Huacaya	raw	black	32
Huacaya	raw	white	12
Huacaya	raw	fawn/beige	32
Huacaya	raw	brown	24
Suri	washed	gray	72
Suri	washed	black	80
Suri	washed	white	40
Suri	washed	fawn/beige	64
Suri	washed	brown	45

use special selectors

There are three other selectors that we want to tell you about. The first is the universal selector, the second is the !important selector, and finally, there's the child selector.

We added another rule to our CSS file, which uses *, which is the universal selector—that is, it applies to every element.

```
* {
    margin: 0;
    padding: 0;
}
```

This rule sets all margins and padding for all elements on the page to zero. Using the universal selector in this fashion is fairly common (to avoid cross-browser incompatibilities), and is referred to as doing a global reset.

The !important selector is the Jedi mind trick of CSS. It tells the browser that this rule, no matter what selectors it uses (or doesn't use) is always the most specific, forcing it (absent any other rules marked !important) to always be applied.

The selector is pronounced "bang important." It's useful when you're having trouble making a specific enough rule to force the particular rule you want to take effect.

```
td {
    padding: 20px !important;
}
```

Lastly, the child selector uses the character >. It targets the immediate child of a given element—that is, if you wanted to apply a rule to all links within a paragraph, so long as that paragraph was within the #mainContent div, you could target them by using the descendent selector #mainContent p a. But what if you wanted that rule to not apply to any blockquotes inside that div? You have paragraphs within the blockquote, and links within the paragraph—so how do you stop it?

You can do that by changing the above selector to #mainContent > p a. That tells the browser that you only want to target links which are inside paragraphs, where those paragraphs are direct descendents of the #mainContent div. If there's a blockquote in between, the rule won't apply. We'll have a specific example of using a child selector in Chapter 7.

style specific elements

extra bits

style a table p. 72

- Most of the selectors we're using in this chapter are supported in current browsers. The main browser that you need to be concerned about is Microsoft Internet Explorer. IE 6 didn't do a good job of supporting CSS2 selectors, and no version of IE supports CSS3 selectors. This table shows which selectors covered in this chapter are supported in various versions of IE, Safari, and Firefox.

Selector	IE6	IE7	IE8	Safari	FF2	FF3	FF3.1
>	N	Y	Y	Y	Y	Y	Y
+	N	Y	Y	Y	Y	Y	Y
:first-child	N	Y	Y	Y	Y	Y	Y
:last-child	N	N	N	Y	Y	Y	Y
:nth-child()	N	N	N	Y	N	N	Y
border-spacing	N	N	Y	Y	Y	Y	Y
border-collapse	Y	Y	Y	Y	Y	Y	Y
:first-letter	N	Y	Y	Y	Y	Y	Y
:hover	N	Y	Y	Y	Y	Y	Y
!important	N	Y	Y	Y	Y	Y	Y

- For the tables, we could have used < th > (table header) cells for the first row instead of < td >, but we wanted to demonstrate how to select and modify something based on first-child.

- If you have two elements, and there are any other elements between where one ends and the other begins, they aren't considered to be adjacent. Using the sidebar navigation as an example (see Chapter 5), the < a > tags are not adjacent to each other, but the < li > tags are.

- The only other valid value for border-collapse is separate.

- Yes, those tr + tr + tr + tr + tr + tr + tr + tr selectors are a pain, because you have to manually set up the formatting for the odd and even rows. But for the foreseeable future, they're the only way to do pure-CSS zebra-striped tables cross-browser without manually setting a class on every other row in the XHTML. The problem with setting classes like that is that you have to remember to set that class whenever you add items to the table. It's more flexible to do it in the CSS.

(continued on next page)

extra bits

style a table (continued)

- There is a difference between tr + tr and tr tr. The former applies to two adjacent rows. The latter would apply to a row inside another row, which would only happen if you had nested tables.

- If you know that you're not going to have to change your table data very often, classes may be the way to go. In that case, you can (for example) add a class = "oddRow" attribute to each odd tr, and then a selector like so: .oddRow { background-color: #EEEEEE; }. And if your data is being generated on the fly by a content management system, this is the approach you should take.

- Another way to target your rules more precisely is to use more specific selectors. For instance, while #mainContent and div#mainContent both target the same element, the latter is more specific. And div#container div#mainContent is even more specific. If you want to very specifically target the class of odd-numbered rows (as just mentioned), you could have your selector be table tr.oddRow { background-color: #EEEEEE; }.

add fancy headings p. 79

- Note that different browsers will interpret rules differently, and will give you different results. For example, the rule font-family: cursive; for the first letter of the heading will give you a quite different look in Safari (top) and Firefox (bottom).

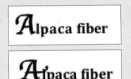

use special selectors p. 80

- Among professional Web designers, it's considered poor form to actually put a site live with !important in a rule—but that doesn't mean it doesn't come in handy when testing. And if you want to use it in your sites, the CSS Police won't come by and make you stop. But !important is considered to be a workaround, not a real solution, so in general, it's preferable to figure out a different way to make all the rules on your site work the way you wanted them to.

style specific elements

7. work better with browsers

As a Web designer, you want your site to look its best, no matter which browser your site visitor is using to view it. There are so many possibilities, from traditional desktop and notebook computers, to smartphones like the iPhone and the BlackBerry, to browsers built into consumer electronics devices like the Sony PlayStation and the Amazon Kindle. And for the future, you should anticipate that browsers will be built into any device with a screen; your television is the obvious next candidate for Web surfing.

To meet the challenge of looking good on any device or browser, there are a few different paths that you can take, and we'll cover them in this chapter. First, we'll show you how to work around some of the many CSS flaws in Microsoft Internet Explorer. Next, you'll see how to take advantage of the extensions to CSS found in newer browsers to get great new effects. And finally, you'll learn how to create special print stylesheets that will help your Web pages look good on that oldest of display devices—the humble sheet of paper.

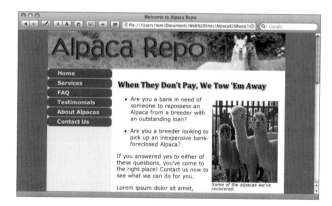

When They Don't Pay, We Tow 'Em Away

- Are you a bank in need of someone to repossess an Alpaca from a breeder with an outstanding loan?

- Are you a breeder looking to pick up an inexpensive bank-foreclosed Alpaca?

If you answered yes to either of these questions, you've come to the right place! Contact us now to see what we can do for you.

Lorem ipsum dolor sit amet, consectetuer adipiscing elit. Praesent aliquam, justo convallis luctus rutrum, erat nulla fermentum diam, at nonummy quam ante ac quam. Maecenas urna purus, fermentum id, molestie in, commodo porttitor, felis. Nam blandit quam ut lacus. Quisque ornare risus quis ligula. Phasellus tristique purus.

Some of the alpacas we've recovered.

adapt for IE

One of the enduring truths of the Web is that because it may be viewed by many different devices, a designer can't always be sure what a page will look like to a given user. That simple fact has led to endless frustration, and that frustration is only compounded when you consider that each browser manufacturer is free to interpret the agreed-upon CSS standards as they see fit. A browser maker may choose to render a particular CSS property differently than other browsers, or indeed not support properties supported by most other browsers.

This brings us to Microsoft Internet Explorer (IE), the most widely used browser in the world. As a Web site author, you can expect the majority of your visitors to be using Internet Explorer 6, 7, or 8. In terms of adherence to CSS standards, in our opinion, IE 6 is terrible, IE 7 fixed many CSS bugs, and IE 8 is still in progress as we write this in early 2009, but it aims for full CSS 2.1 compatibility.

Most people are using IE 7 (approximately 50% of all users, as of Q4 2008), with another 20% still using IE 6. So that means that a significant percentage of your site's vistors will be using browsers that don't render CSS correctly. If you want your site to work well with IE, there are some workarounds that you must implement.

Adapting your pages for IE involves two parts. The first part is simple: it's just a bit of conditional XHTML. That's some XHTML that is wrapped in XHTML comment tags, so that it is only executed by Internet Explorer. The second part is CSS that takes advantage of the conditional XHTML.

The conditional XHTML is straightforward, with an easily understood syntax.

```
<!--[if IE]>
    Any XHTML here that you want
<![endif]-->
```

The XHTML comment begins and contains the [if IE] statement. At the end of the XHTML, there's another comment tag that contains the [endif] statement. This is a Microsoft-only thing, and only IE 5 or later will understand it as an instruction to pay attention to the XHTML inside the comment tags. However, because it appears to be a simple XHTML comment to all other browsers, your page is still valid.

On the Alpaca Repo site, we've put this conditional XHTML near the top of each page (between < body > and < div id = "container" >):

```
<!--[if IE]>
    <div id="IEroot">
<![endif]-->
```

and this near the end (between < /div > and < /body >):

```
<!--[if IE]>
    </div>
<![endif]-->
```

All this does is check to see if you're running any version of IE. If you are, you'll get an extra div called #IEroot around #container. If you aren't, you won't.

We're using Adobe Dreamweaver's handy ability to show the boxes on a page in different colors. The conditional XHTML creates a new div, #IEroot, around #container, but only in IE.

adapt for IE (cont.)

Now that we've wrapped a new div around the whole page for IE users, we need to write some CSS that targets that div. To show that, we'll use a modification of one of the table examples in Chapter 6. We took one of the tables from Chapter 6 and styled it one way for non-IE browsers and another for IE. Remember how we said in that chapter that IE can't handle last-child and IE through version 7 doesn't handle border-spacing? Well, this works around that—the non-IE browsers get the better versions, and IE gets the older stuff.

In our CSS, we need a way to target elements on the page if the user is employing one of the more capable browsers, such as Firefox and Safari, and a different way to target those elements if the page is being viewed in IE.

To do that, we'll use the > operator, which is the child selector. A child selector targets an immediate child of a certain element. In other words, the child selector lets you set rules that are only applied when a particular element is directly inside another element you specify.

Here's how we're using it. If we want to write some CSS just for IE, all we have to do now is write:

```
#IEroot #myTable {
    border-collapse: collapse;
}
```

The end result of that is that you get a rule that only ever applies to IE. In a nutshell: all you have to do is add #IEroot before your rule, and it becomes an IE-only rule.

The reverse side of that is that you can add non-IE rules as well, just by writing, say:

```
body > #container #myTable {
    border-spacing: 6px;
}
```

This works because the #container div is an immediate child of body only for non-IE browsers.

This can be a little puzzling, so a diagram of the structure of the XHTML file can help.

This is the structure seen by Internet Explorer.

This is the structure that non-IE browsers see.

Here's the CSS, first for the more capable browsers, such as Firefox and Safari:

```css
body > #container #fiberChart {
    border-spacing: 6px;
}

body > #container #fiberChart tr:hover {
    background-color: #BAE8BF;
}

body > #container #fiberChart td:last-child {
    text-align: right;
}
```

These rules contain selectors that IE doesn't handle, such as border-spacing and last-child. As a result, the CSS can be relatively short.

work better with browsers   **87**

adapt for IE (cont.)

For IE, the CSS is more extensive:

```
#IEroot #fiberChart td+td+td+td {
    text-align: right;
}

#IEroot #fiberChart {
    border-collapse: collapse;
}

#IEroot #fiberChart tr+tr+tr,
#IEroot #fiberChart tr+tr+tr+tr+tr,
#IEroot #fiberChart tr+tr+tr+tr+tr+tr+tr,
#IEroot #fiberChart tr+tr+tr+tr+tr+tr+tr+tr+tr,
#IEroot #fiberChart tr+tr+tr+tr+tr+tr+tr+tr+tr+tr+tr {
    background-color: #EEEEEE;
    border-bottom: 2px #006600 solid;
}

#IEroot #fiberChart tr+tr,
#IEroot #fiberChart tr+tr+tr+tr,
#IEroot #fiberChart tr+tr+tr+tr+tr+tr,
#IEroot #fiberChart tr+tr+tr+tr+tr+tr+tr+tr,
#IEroot #fiberChart tr+tr+tr+tr+tr+tr+tr+tr+tr+tr {
    background-color: #BAE8BF;
    border-bottom-width: 0;
}
```

In these rules, we're selecting the #IEroot div, then acting on only the elements within that div. Because the div is created by the conditional XHTML only in IE, the rules only take effect in IE, and are ignored by other browsers. The actual work being done by these rules is very similar to the way we formatted tables in Chapter 6; take a look there if you need an explanation of how these rules work.

The results of this table formatting are different by design; we could have made the CSS produce equivalent results, but we prefer to show you how to achieve two different looks.

Alpaca Fiber for sale

Type	Condition	Color	$/lb.
Huacaya	raw	gray	48
Huacaya	raw	black	32
Huacaya	raw	white	12
Huacaya	raw	fawn/beige	32
Huacaya	raw	brown	24
Suri	washed	gray	72
Suri	washed	black	80
Suri	washed	white	40
Suri	washed	fawn/beige	64
Suri	washed	brown	45

The table as formatted in Internet Explorer.

Alpaca Fiber for sale

Type	Condition	Color	$/lb.
Huacaya	raw	gray	48
Huacaya	raw	black	32
Huacaya	raw	white	12
Huacaya	raw	fawn/beige	32
Huacaya	raw	brown	24
Suri	washed	gray	72
Suri	washed	black	80
Suri	washed	white	40
Suri	washed	fawn/beige	64
Suri	washed	brown	45

The table as formatted in Firefox.

use browser extensions

Ever since the Web became a popular medium in the mid-1990s, Web site designers constantly pushed the boundaries and limitations of XHTML to create pages that reflected their vision. This desire to do more with Web pages eventually led to the creation of CSS and XHTML and their standardization by the W3C, the World Wide Web Consortium. But as the Web became more complex, the pace of standards change by the W3C has slowed to a crawl. The currently accepted, widely supported version of CSS, CSS 2.1, has still not become a final and official standard (as of January 2009), and the next standard, CSS3, has been in the works since 1998, with no final resolution in sight.

On the Alpaca Repo site, we've used a CSS3 property, text-shadow (only supported by Safari and Firefox 3.1 or later), and applied it to all the headings.

```
h1, h2, h3, h4, h5, h6 {
    font-family: Cambria, "Palatino Linotype", "Book Antiqua",
                 "URW Palladio L", serif;
    text-shadow: #444444 2px 2px 4px;
}
```

The text-shadow property has the values color, x-offset, y-offset, blur-radius.

The result, shown in Safari, shows the subtle shadow added to the heading.

Our services

Alpaca Fiber for sale

Type	Condition	Color	$/lb.
Huacaya	raw	gray	48
Huacaya	raw	black	32

We also added text-shadow to the button text in the sidebar, both in the normal state and in the hover state.

```
#sidebar a {
    text-shadow: #264C4C 2px 2px 4px;
}

#sidebar a:hover {
    text-shadow: #264C4C 1px 1px 2px;
}
```

The result looks like this:

Although the W3C moves slowly, browser manufacturers are sensitive to the desires of their customers. Consequently, over the years, they have produced a variety of browser extensions, which are CSS properties that are understood by a particular browser, and not by other browsers. We've seen extensions for Firefox, Safari, and Internet Explorer. These extensions add any number of abilities to the CSS rendered by these browsers. For example, many extensions provide selectors and properties that are expected to be included in the eventual CSS3 standard. Others, especially some of the Apple extensions, add stylistic tweaks that allow Web sites to more closely mimic Mac OS X user interface elements.

browser extensions (cont.)

Browser makers have implemented these extensions with care, however. They don't want designers to start to use extensions, and then later get messed up when the standard actually does ship and the syntax has changed. So they've come up with a convention that will protect developers' work in the future. If a browser maker does add something non-standard, they start its name off with a dash, followed by the vendor name.

One of the nicest bits about browser-specific CSS is that if you're on the page with anything other than that specific browser, there's absolutely no effect, positive or negative. So if you're designing your page to look really cool in Firefox, for instance, you don't have to worry about these properties screwing up other browsers.

You probably noticed the rounded corners on the buttons in the sidebar; we produced those (supported in Safari and Firefox 3 and later) with the border-radius property, with specific versions for each browser. In these declarations, webkit refers to the Web rendering engine built into Safari, and moz is a reference to the Mozilla Foundation, the sponsors of the open-source Firefox browser.

```
#sidebar a {
    -webkit-border-radius: 10px;
    -moz-border-radius: 10px;
}
```

work better with browsers

add print stylesheets

There's a tendency to think of the Web as a medium that only appears on screens, whether it be the screen of a computer or a mobile device. But the Web is a flexible and useful medium, and people often want to print hard copies of Web pages for reference or even for archival purposes. However, often when you print a Web page, there is a lot of the page that you just don't need in the printed document. For example, you probably don't need the Web page's navigation bar, and you might not need some of the images on the page either. With CSS, you can create a special stylesheet that only takes effect when the page is printed, and omits the information that you don't want to print.

This page keeps the logo at the top of the page, but eliminates the navigation bar and changes the margins of the page to work better in the printed form.

add print stylesheets (cont.)

To begin creating a print stylesheet, you'll need to link the new stylesheet, which we're calling printStyle.css, in the XHTML of your page, as we discussed in Chapter 1.

< link rel = "stylesheet" href = "printStyle.css" type = "text/css" media = "print" />

< link rel = "stylesheet" href = "printStyle.css" type = "text/css" media = "print,handheld" />

As an alternative, this second example includes the handheld media type, because handheld devices (the major exception being the iPhone; see the extra bits for more information) often have browsers that can't handle the complexities of modern Web pages well, and so a simplified representation is more appropriate.

Next, in each of the following rules in the CSS file, all we're doing, really, is backing out something that was done in the main styles.css file.

```
#container {
    width: 100%;
}
```

Here we reset the width of #container from 80% to 100%, because we don't want the big side borders when we print.

```
#sidebar {
    display: none;
}
```

When we print, we also don't need to see the navigation.

```
#mainContent {
    margin-left: 0;
}
```

In the online version, we set a large left margin on #mainContent so that it doesn't overwrite the navigation. We need to turn that off for the print version.

```
h1, h2, h3, h4, h5, h6 {
    text-shadow: #444444 0 0 0;
}
```

Finally, shadows don't look good when printing, so we want to get rid of them, too.

extra bits

adapt for IE p. 84

- Just because IE 8 is aiming for full CSS 2.1 compatibility doesn't mean that it will do everything you might want to do. Some of the more advanced CSS selectors (and some of what we've included in this book) are part of the still-emerging CSS3 standard, which has been in progress since 2001. Because it has been gestating so long, browser makers have decided to pick and choose the most useful bits of the standard and build support for those pieces into their browsers. Firefox, Safari, and Google Chrome all have partial CSS3 support. IE 8 does not.

- There are many sites and books that teach you how to work around specific bugs or other problems with IE. This isn't one of them. We're focusing on how you can generally write alternative CSS for IE, and how you can create additional rules that work only in IE.

- This trick with the comment tags can be used to put in any kind of XHTML you want, not just divs. Some people use this to bring in IE-only CSS. Some, to bring in IE-only JavaScript.

- With our conditional XHTML, we're just checking to see if the browser is IE. But you can get much more advanced with IE-specific conditionals. See http://msdn.microsoft.com/en-us/library/ms537512(VS.85).aspx for more details.

- In the CSS, you can put any element into the selector after #IEroot or #container; given that we're using descendent selectors, it will find those elements anywhere they are within the document.

use browser extensions p. 90

- You can find out more about browser extensions from the developer sites for Mozilla (for Firefox: http://developer.mozilla.org/en/CSS_Reference/Mozilla_Extensions) and Apple (for Safari: http://developer.apple.com/documentation/AppleApplications/Reference/SafariCSSRef/Articles/StandardCSSProperties .html).

- When properties currently specified as browser extensions are standardized, designers should be able to just take off the -vendor at the beginning of the property name, assuming that the browser makers chose a good design in the first place. If not, designers will also have to fix the syntax, but the old stuff (that is, the stuff with the dash-name) should still work.

work better with browsers

add print stylesheets p. 93

- There are many media types, and though we're focusing on the one most commonly used, print, it is just one of them. This table includes them all.

all	Suitable for all devices. If no media type is used, this is the default.
braille	Intended for Braille tactile feedback devices.
embossed	Intended for paged Braille printers.
handheld	Intended for handheld devices (small screen, limited bandwidth).
print	Intended for paged material and for documents viewed on screen in print preview mode.
projection	Intended for projected presentations, for example projectors.
screen	Intended primarily for color computer screens.
speech or aural	Intended for speech synthesizers.
tty	Intended for media using a fixed-pitch character grid (such as teletypes). Authors should not use pixel units with this media type.
tv	Intended for television-type devices (low resolution, color, limited-scrollability screens, sound available).

- When you're working with print stylesheets, you can sometimes preview how your page will print. Tell Safari/Mac you want to print, and the Print dialog shows how it will appear when it's printed—you don't actually have to waste the paper while making sure your page looks good. Or tell Firefox/Mac to print, then just click Preview in the following dialog. On Safari for Windows, use the File > Print Preview menu choice to see how your printed page will look.

(continued on next page)

add print stylesheets (cont.)

- The Safari browser in the iPhone is, for our purposes, identical to the Safari browser in desktop versions of Mac OS X or Windows. It doesn't identify itself with the handheld media type, and Web pages look pretty much the same as they do in Safari on the desktop.

- If there was anything else that we wanted to get rid of or not see when printing, we could add a rule for that with display:none as well. On the other hand, if there was something we wanted to show only when we were printing, we could put it on the main stylesheet with display:none and then use display:block in this stylesheet to make it print.

8. add to your site

Now that your site is mostly complete, it's time to start thinking about some of the options that you have in terms of layout and content. Earlier in this book, we purposely designed a relatively simple site, figuring that you will dress it up as you see fit, as well as to match your personal artistic vision.

In this chapter, we will explore methods to change and add to the site. For example, instead of the two-column layout that we've used until now, you might prefer a three-column layout, with the third column reserved for additional links (like a blogroll) or to add advertising content. You might want to change the navigation bar from vertical in the left-hand sidebar to a horizontal menu bar under the header. And if you have a more complex site structure, you will want to know how to turn either a vertical or horizontal navigation bar into a true menu bar, with multiple menu choices under a main choice. All of these are changes that you can make easily, with just a few changes to the site's existing XHTML and CSS.

create horizontal menu

This chapter is all about taking one XHTML file and changing its appearance dramatically using almost entirely CSS, with minimal XHTML changes. The main thing that we will change in the XHTML from previous chapters is that we will rename the div that contained the navigation bar. In all of the previous chapters we called it #sidebar, and in this chapter we will rename it #navbar, since in some of the examples the navigation bar won't be on the side of the layout.

In this particular example, we'll show you how to turn the vertical navigation bar that was inside the left-hand sidebar into a horizontal navigation bar that is snug underneath the header. Because it isn't needed anymore, the left-hand sidebar will go away.

In order to make the changes to the navigation bar, we'll need to change the CSS rules for the following:

- The position and color of the navbar div.

- The look of the anchor tags inside the navbar.

- The behavior of the anchor tags when the user hovers over them.

- And finally, we'll have to change the #mainContent div a bit, since the left-hand sidebar will no longer exist.

add to your site

To begin, let's review the old CSS
from previous chapters:

Replace that with this new CSS:

```
#navbar {
    float: left;
    width: 12em;
    font-weight: bold;
}
```

```
#navbar {
    font-weight: bold;
    height: 1.8em;
    background-color: #336666;
    overflow: hidden;
}
```

The font-weight is still bold in both snippets, but everything else has changed. We don't need float: left, because we no longer want the entire menu to be left-aligned. And because this is a horizontal menu, rather than a vertical one, we eliminate the width property in favor of height.

We're setting the background-color here because we want the entire horizontal span to be the same color (which we didn't when it was vertical). We set overflow: hidden so that the menu won't do freaky things when the user changes the width of the browser window to be very narrow.

Now let's change the look of the links in the navbar.

Here's the old CSS:

```
#navbar a {
    display: block;
    background-color: #336666;
    border-bottom: 1px #EBEBEB solid;
    padding: 3px 3px 5px 30px;
    color: #EBEBEB;
    text-decoration: none;
}
```

create horizontal menu (cont.)

That CSS needs to be replaced with this new rule:

```
#navbar a {
    float: left;
    white-space: nowrap;
    border-right: 1px #EBEBEB solid;
    padding: 3px 15px 4px 15px;
    color: #EBEBEB;
    text-decoration: none;
}
```

Again, some things (color and text-decoration) remain the same. Let's go through the changes.

By applying the float: left at the level of the anchor (instead of at the div level), it makes each link stack up to the right of the previous menu item. The white-space: nowrap property, which is new to us, acts like the XHTML non-breaking space entity . In other words, it keeps the words inside the anchor tag from wrapping. We don't want our menu items to wrap, so nowrap does the trick.

The old CSS used border-bottom to create a horizontal line between the menu items. The new CSS uses border-right to create a vertical line between the menu items. We also adjusted the padding, using trial and error to make everything look right.

To change the behavior of the links when a user hovers over them, we only need make a few minor changes. Once again, let's compare the old and new CSS.

Out with the old:

```
#navbar a:hover {
    background-color: #EBEBEB;
    color: #336666;
    border-right: 3px #999999 solid;
    border-bottom: 3px #999999 solid;
    padding-bottom: 3px;
}
```

And in with the new:

The only changes when we hover over the link are the the addition of some padding on the right and the size of the padding on the bottom of the menu item.

```
#navbar a:hover {
    background-color: #EBEBEB;
    color: #336666;
    border-right: 3px #999999 solid;
    border-bottom: 3px #999999 solid;
    padding-right: 13px;
    padding-bottom: 1px;
}
```

The last change that we need to make is to the #mainContent div.

The old CSS:

This gets replaced with the new CSS:

```
#mainContent {
    background-color:
        #FFFFFF;
    margin-left: 12em;
    padding: 10px 20px 0 1em;
}
```

```
#mainContent {
    background-color:
        #FFFFFF;
    padding: 10px 20px 0 1em;
}
```

All we need to do here is eliminate the big left margin where the sidebar used to be.

bring back left column

Let's say that you like the look of the horizontal menu under the header, but you would still like to maintain a left sidebar, perhaps so that you can put advertising content there.

Ad banner ———

Sidebar ———

To create this effect, we used the same CSS as in the preceding example, and we added the following rules:

```
#sidebar {
    float: left;
    width: 12em;
    text-align: center;
    padding-top: 20px;
}

#sidebar img {
    border-width: 0;
}
```

This CSS brings back the left-hand sidebar, which we're now using to show that vertical ad banner. The #sidebar img selector sets the ad banner's border-width to zero, so that the image doesn't have the blue line around it indicating a link.

add to your site

Because we brought back the sidebar, we also need to adjust the #mainContent div.

```
#mainContent {
    background-color: #FFFFFF;
    margin-left: 12em;
    padding: 10px 20px 0 1em;
}
```

And again, this looks just like the #mainContent area in the styles that we used in the preceding chapters in this book.

As for the XHTML, all that needs to be done is add a #sidebar div, which can then contain anything you want on the side of your page.

add top ad banner

In the last section, we saw how to put an advertising banner in the left sidebar. Another very common place for an ad banner is at the top of the page, above the page header.

Adding the ad banner requires adding a new div to the XHTML, called #adHeader. The div goes right at the beginning of #container and right before #header.

```
<div id="container">
   <div id="adHeader">
      <a href="http://www.pixel.mu"><img
         src="images/pixelHorizontal.jpg" width="468"
         height="60" alt="ad banner" /></a>
   </div> <!-- end #adHeader -->
   <div id="header">
      <img src="images/header.jpg" width="800" height="110"
         alt="site header" />
   </div> <!-- end #header -->
```

As you can see, the #adHeader div contains a link tag that points to the destination the user will go to if they click on the ad (in this case, it's our cat's Web site).

The only additions we need to make to the CSS file for the site are two rules, one of which centers and pads the ad banner and the other which suppresses the blue line around the graphic.

```css
#adHeader {
    text-align: center;
    padding: 10px;
}

#adHeader img {
    border-width: 0;
}
```

add third column

In this variation of our site, we'll have the header at the top, the navigation bar on the left, and the usual main content area, but we'll add a third column on the right side of the page that contains links to other sites and also a vertical ad box. Instead of another mockup ad for our cat, we'll use a real ad box that is generated by Amazon.com, using a snippet of code they provide.

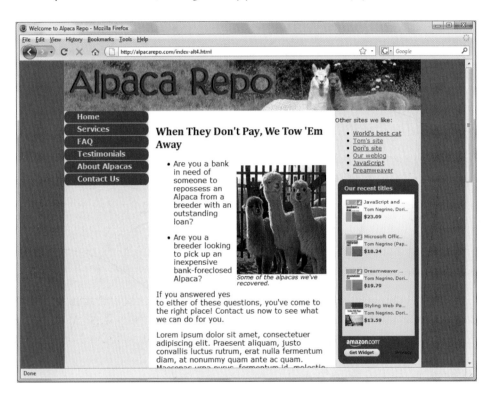

To add a third column, we'll need to make additions to both the XHTML and the CSS. Let's begin with the XHTML, by adding a new div called #adbar.

```
<div id="adbar">
    <p>Other sites we like:</p><ul>
    <li><a href="http://www.pixel.mu">World's best cat</a></li>
    <li><a href="http://www.negrino.com">Tom's site</a></li>
    <li><a href="http://www.dori.com">Dori's site</a></li>
    <li><a href="http://www.backupbrain.com">Our weblog
        </a></li>
    <li><a href="http://www.javascriptworld.com">JavaScript
        </a></li>
    <li><a href="http://www.dreamweaverbook.com">Dreamweaver
        </a></li>
    </ul>
    <script type="text/javascript" src="http://ws.amazon.com/wi
dgets/q?ServiceVersion=20070822&amp;MarketPlace=US&amp;ID=V20
070822/US/chalcedonyconsul/8001/2e92b15b-dfaa-46b0-bcfe-09c7d
4b58575">
    </script>
</div>  <!-- end #adbar -->
```

Inside the div, we've added an unordered list with links to our related sites. Then we've done something new: adding a <script> tag. This one call to JavaScript in the XHTML required no programming knowledge; all we did was fill out a form on Amazon's site, which generated the <script> tag for us, which we then copied and pasted into the XHTML.

To position the div, we added the following CSS:

add third column (cont.)

```css
#adbar {
    float: right;
    width: 15em;
    font-size: .8em;
}

#adbar div {
    margin: 0 auto;
}
```

You might be wondering: why use 15em on the right column when the left column has a width of 12em—shouldn't they be equal? The answer is: actually, they are. The trick is that when an element's width is declared using relative sizes, in order to figure out the actual width of the element, the browser uses the size of the text contained in that element. The text inside #adbar is .8em, or, 80% of the size used on the rest of the page. If we multiply 15em by .8em, the result is 12em—or in other words, the left and right columns are the same width.

Giving the div inside #adbar a margin of 0 auto allowed us to make the Amazon widget always be centered. We use the same trick on #container way back in Chapter 2.

We also added one declaration to the #mainContent rule:

```css
#mainContent {
    background-color: #FFFFFF;
    margin-right: 12em;
    margin-left: 12em;
    padding: 10px 20px 0 1em;
}
```

We added the margin-right property to make room for the right column. Here, we used 12em rather than 15em because the number is calculated based on the text size inside #mainContent.

add to your site

add fly-out menus

Up to this point in the book, we've made the assumption that the Alpaca Repo site will have a very simple navigation bar; just a simple group of links, all on the same level. But if your site has a more complex structure, you're going to want to include a more involved menu bar, one that can handle secondary choices.

If all common Web browsers were fully standards compliant, you would be able to implement these sorts of complex menu structures using nothing more than XHTML and CSS. Unfortunately, the dominant browser, Microsoft Internet Explorer, doesn't properly handle all the required CSS. So instead, we'll use the triple threat of XHTML, CSS, and JavaScript to create menus that will work in almost any browser in widespread use today.

We're not going to try to teach you JavaScript; this isn't that kind of book. But we don't have to, because our menus will be made with the help of jQuery, a JavaScript toolkit. JavaScript toolkits are pre-written, already-programmed libraries of functions that make it easy for you to bring the power of JavaScript to your projects. In this particular example, jQuery provides the horsepower to actually make the menus work. All we will need to do is plug the names of the divs and tags in our XHTML document into a prewritten script.

add fly-out menus (cont.)

We'll need to add two < script > tags to the XHTML, which will go between the < head > and < /head > tags.

The first < script > tag loads the jQuery code, hosted (in this example) on one of Google's servers. See the extra bits for a discussion of serving jQuery.

```
<script type="text/javascript" src="http://ajax.googleapis.com
/ajax/libs/jquery/1.2.6/jquery.js"></script>
```

The next script includes references to the specific parts of our XHTML page, so that jQuery can use them to implement the menus.

```
<script type="text/javascript">
    $(document).ready(function() {
        $("#navbar li ul").hide();

        $("#navbar li").hover(
            function() {
                $(this).children("ul").show();
            },
            function() {
                $(this).children("ul").hide();
            });   //hover
    });         // document ready
</script>
```

If you look inside the parenthesis at the jQuery code, it should look vaguely familiar. That's because jQuery is very CSS-like in the way it handles selectors. That is, when the jQuery code uses "#navbar li ul", it means exactly the same thing it does in CSS: we want something to apply to all uls inside all lis inside #navbar.

add to your site

The XHTML that makes up the menu is not much more complex than what we've used in previous chapters. It is still an unordered list, but now it includes nested unordered lists for the second-level menu choices.

```
<div id="navbar">
   <ul>
      <li><a href="index.html">Home</a></li>
      <li><a href="">Services</a>
         <ul>
            <li><a href="recovery.html">Alpaca Recovery
               </a></li>
            <li><a href="preown.html">Pre-owned Alpaca sales
               </a></li>
            <li><a href="fiber.html">Alpaca fiber</a></li>
         </ul>
      </li>
      <li><a href="">FAQ</a>
         <ul>
            <li><a href="recoveryfaq.html">Recovery FAQ
               </a></li>
            <li><a href="salesfaq.html">Sales FAQ</a></li>
         </ul>
      </li>
      <li><a href="">Testimonials</a>
         <ul>
            <li><a href="fi_blurb.html">Financial
               Institutions</a></li>
            <li><a href="breeder_blurb.html">Breeders</a></li>
            <li><a href="broker_blurb.html">Brokers</a></li>
         </ul>
      </li>
      <li><a href="about.html">About Alpacas</a></li>
      <li><a href="contact.html">Contact Us</a></li>
   </ul>
</div> <!-- end #navbar -->
```

add fly-out menus (cont.)

The CSS changes for navbar are minimal:

The only difference here is that the last value of padding used to be 30px and now it's 10px. That is, we moved the text over to the left to provide more room for the fly-outs on the right. We also got rid of the radial corners that appear in Firefox and Safari, because they don't look good with fly-out menus.

```css
#navbar a {
    display: block;
    padding: 3px 3px 5px 10px;
    background-color: #336666;
    color: #EBEBEB;
    border-bottom: 1px #EBEBEB solid;
    text-decoration: none;
}
```

To style the fly-out menus, we create a rule that selects list items that are inside list items.

```css
#navbar li li {
    white-space: nowrap;
    width: 15em;
    margin-left: 20px;
    position: relative;
}
```

As we've previously done, we use white-space set to nowrap so that our menu items won't ever break in the middle (which would look bad). Giving the element a width makes them all be the same dimensions. Otherwise, they'd all only be as wide as they need to be (which would again look really bad). The left margin of 20px makes the second-level items stand off a tad from the main menu items. And finally, making this element be position:relative tells the browser to make these block elements, which keeps the underlying text from showing through the buttons.

add horizontal fly-outs

Looking back to the first task in this chapter, create horizontal menu, you might be thinking "That looks nice, but what if my site has a more complex menu structure?" You've come to the right place, as this example shows you how to add second-level menu choices to a horizontal navbar.

The XHTML for this example is identical to that in add fly-out menus, so we're going to focus just on the CSS changes. This task also makes use of the jQuery scripts to power the menus. Refer to the previous task if you need more information on either the XHTML or jQuery.

We're going to need to change the #navbar rule that styles anchor tags that we used in create horizontal menu, so let's review it.

We replace that rule with the following two rules:

```
#navbar a {
    float: left;
    white-space: nowrap;
    padding:
        3px 15px 4px 15px;
    border-right:
        1px #EBEBEB solid;
    text-decoration: none;
    color: #EBEBEB;
}
```

```
#navbar li {
    float: left;
    white-space: nowrap;
    padding:
        3px 15px 4px 15px;
    border-right:
        1px #EBEBEB solid;
}

#navbar a {
    text-decoration: none;
    color: #EBEBEB;
}
```

add horizontal fly-outs (cont.)

What you should be able to see here is that the rules that used to be applied to the links inside the #navbar are now split into two: some stayed with the links, but others were moved to the list items. That's because we want the fly-outs to appear when you're over the entire list item, not just the link itself.

Similarly, we need to split up the a:hover rule into three new rules.

First, the old rule:

```
#navbar a:hover {
    background-color:
        #EBEBEB;
    color: #336666;
    border-right:
        3px #999999 solid;
    border-bottom:
        3px #999999 solid;
    padding-right: 13px;
    padding-bottom: 1px;
}
```

And now the new rules:

```
#navbar li:hover {
    background-color:
        #EBEBEB;
    border-right:
        3px #999999 solid;
    border-bottom:
        3px #999999 solid;
    padding-right: 13px;
    padding-bottom: 1px;
}

#navbar li:hover > a {
    color: #336666;
}

#navbar ul ul {
    position: fixed;
    background-color:
        #336666;
    margin-top: 4px;
    margin-left: -15px;
    border-top:
        1px #EBEBEB solid;
}
```

Again, properties that used to be applied to links are now applied to list items. In the first of the new rules, the only property that didn't get carried over from the old rule was the text color; that's in the second rule, directly below. That rule also uses the child selector (>), as we want to only change the text color on the button over which we're hovering, and not on the fly-out buttons.

And finally, we have some rules that apply to the uls inside uls (that is, only the fly-outs). The only ones that are really of interest are the top and left margins, which align the child buttons under their parent.

add to your site

create standard menus

Our last site variation builds on the horizontal menus from the immediately pre-ceding task, but instead of the second-level menu choices flying out as another bar below the main horizontal navigation bar, we've changed the CSS so that the second-level items drop down vertically, just like a standard menu bar.

All we need to do is make a small change to one rule, and add one more.

The rule that needs to be changed is for #navbar ul ul, and that change is to remove the top border, because now it needs to be between individual menu items instead of above the fly-out menu.

```
#navbar ul ul {
    position: fixed;
    background-color:
        #336666;
    margin-top: 4px;
    margin-left: -15px;
}
```

Here's the rule that we need to add:

```
#navbar li li {
    float: none;
    padding-right: 16px;
    border-right-width: 0;
    border-top:
        1px #EBEBEB solid;
}
```

That, by itself, is enough to make the menus go down instead of across. The trick is that in the previous example, the menu items inherited the float left from their parent, so they went across in the same way. In order to make them go vertically, we need to get them to stop floating by setting float to none. Doing that gets the effect we want.

extra bits

create horizontal menu p. 100

- Here are the possible values for the white-space property:

Value	Description
nowrap	Keep lines of text from breaking
pre	Acts just like the HTML < pre > tag (for preformatted text)
normal	The default

add third column p. 108

- This particular advertisement came from http://widgets .amazon.com/Amazon-My-Favorites-Widget. All you have to do is sign up as an Amazon associate, fill out the form, and you'll get a snippet to add to your web page.

- If you prefer Google ads instead (or additionally), you can get those by signing up at http:// adsense.google.com.

add fly-out menus p. 111

- There are many JavaScript tool-kits available, and jQuery is just one of them. We like it because it's lightweight, which means that sites using it load more

quickly; it has an active develop-ment community; it has a plug-in architecture (so that if jQuery itself doesn't do a particular func-tion that you want, chances are someone has written it as a plug-in), and it's fairly easy to use for people who know CSS, but are less comfortable with JavaScript.

- If you want, you can download jQuery from jquery.com and install it on your own Web server. We've chosen instead to use a copy of jQuery that is freely hosted by Google at http://ajax .googleapis.com. By doing this, we're taking advantage of their fast servers.

- We said that we weren't going to try to teach you JavaScript in this book. But that doesn't mean that we're not ready to teach you JavaScript if you want to learn more. We're happy to recom-mend one of our other books, JavaScript and Ajax for the Web, Seventh Edition: Visual Quick-Start Guide, also published by the fine folks at Peachpit Press.

- Some browsers, like Mobile Safari on the iPhone, don't support :hover. You'll need to make sure that any menus you create are still accessible (ours are).

9. troubleshoot and learn more

Congratulations! As you have worked through this book, you've been building a modern Web site with separate content and style using XHTML and CSS. And with the techniques in Chapter 8, you should have been able to customize our simple Alpaca Repo example for your own needs.

Along the way, you've seen how CSS works, and you have probably run into a few situations where it didn't. If you're anything like us, you made a typo or two while writing CSS, and it took you a little while to figure out why your page wasn't acting the way you expected. This is completely normal; after all, CSS can be a tricky beast. In this chapter, we'll focus on tools that you can use to troubleshoot your CSS, and then we'll point you at some resources where you can learn more about CSS on your own.

validate your css

One of the easiest ways to track down problems with your CSS is to validate it to check for errors. You validate your CSS by running it through an online tool sponsored by the W3C (the standards body for CSS and XHTML). You can find that tool at http://jigsaw.w3.org/css-validator/. When you go to that page, you have the choice of validating a Web address, uploading a CSS file to the service, or copying and pasting CSS directly into the page.

We find that it's usually easiest to click the By URI tab, enter a Web address, and click the Check button. The system is smart enough to find and check all the linked style sheets for the address you enter.

After validation, you'll get a report that tells you if you have any problems with your CSS.

If you do, consider whether you're validating against the proper version of CSS. The validation tool defaults to CSS 2.1, but the CSS that we checked here contains CSS3 elements, which is why some errors were reported.

To change the CSS version the tool uses, click the More Options link, then choose the CSS level you want from the Profile pop-up menu before you click the Check button.

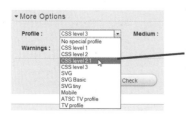

get debugging tools

Sometimes you can have valid CSS but you're still not getting the results you would like on your pages. Oftentimes, this is because you have errors that validation tools can't catch. For example, a capitalization typo on an ID won't be caught by the validator—that is, the elements #mainContent and #maincontent are not the same thing but the validator won't catch this. In cases like this, a debugging tool that runs in the browser can help.

Our two favorite CSS debugging extensions both run under Firefox. The first is called Firebug, and you can get it at http://getfirebug.com/.

The other is the Web Developer toolbar (not shown), which you can download from http://chrispederick.com/work/web-developer/.

Once you install the extensions into Firefox, each plug-in gives you a large suite of tools for inspecting and editing CSS.

We also suggest that you download and install the XRAY bookmarklet, from WestCiv (http://www.westciv.com/xray/), which works in all modern browsers, and allows you to inspect the properties of elements on a page.

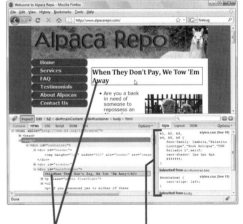

Highlighted element on the page and in XHTML

Styles affecting the highlighted element

debug css

There's one more debugging tool that we didn't mention in the last section, because you don't have to install it. It's called the Web Inspector, and it comes with recent versions of Safari. You activate it by choosing Safari > Preferences > Advanced, then click "Show Develop menu in menu bar." Then choose Develop > Show Web Inspector. Alternately, you can right-click on the problem area and choose "Inspect Element" from the contextual menu.

The main thing that you want to do with any of these debugging tools is inspect elements on your page to see what rules affect the element. For example, we've selected the Home button of the Alpaca Repo site in Safari's Web Inspector (opposite, left) and Firebug (right) to show you how each tool shows you the same information, but in slightly different ways.

Some errors you're likely to run into:

- If an element has a numeric value other than zero, the measurement unit must be specified. It also can't contain any spaces; that is, you have to use 20px not 20 px or 20.

- Check to see if you're missing any semicolons. While they're optional on the last declaration in a block, you do need it on all others—so it's good practice to just always use it.

- Make sure that all your quotes, parenthesis, and braces are properly closed.

- You can't be too careful about typos! There can be a big difference between body.usualStyle, body usualStyle, and body .usualStyle.

By inspecting elements that aren't working the way you want, you can usually figure out what's wrong, and fix the problem. If you're still having trouble, try simplifying your buggy page. Make a standalone page that showcases the issue—that is, add the CSS to the page itself. Then, try deleting things one by one (both CSS and XHTML) and see if the problem still exists. If the problem goes away, add the bit back in that you just deleted, and try deleting something else. Eventually, you should get to the point where everything on the page either causes the problem, or is needed to demonstrate the problem.

Safari gives you one extra little bit of possibly useful information: all of the currently applied style rules combined into one "Computed styles" section.

While Safari and Firefox display color rules differently, they both actually mean the same thing and produce the same result.

These are the border radius values that Firefox understands.

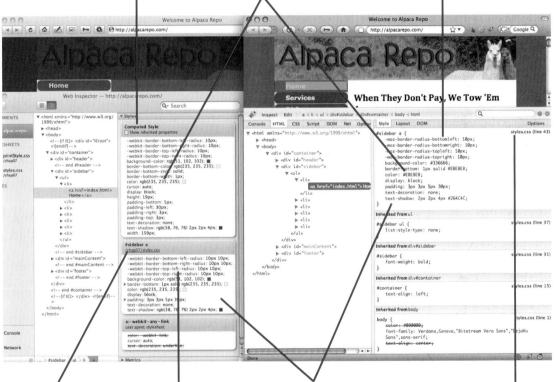

This tells you where Safari is getting its style information from.

These are the border radius values that Safari understands.

Note that overall, these declarations are the same, or at least work out to the same thing.

This tells you where Firefox is getting its style information from.

learn more about css

Here are some sites that we think are good places to learn more about CSS.

CSS tutorials, info and help:

- WestCiv sells a commercial product, but they also give away a lot of information as well.
  http://www.westciv.com/style_master/house/

- Position Is Everything is a site that explains CSS bugs in modern browsers, provides demo examples of CSS behaviors, and shows how to "make it work."
  http://www.positioniseverything.net

Resource Lists: These two sites are just lists of links, but they're well-chosen.

- Web Design References: Cascading Style Sheets
  http://www.d.umn.edu/itss/support/Training/Online/webdesign/css.html

- CSS Resources from Website Tips
  http://websitetips.com/css/

Some useful extras:

- Browser support for CSS: This tells you which browsers support which CSS features.
  http://www.westciv.com/style_master/academy/browser_support/

- CSS specificity: For the crazy person who wants to actually understand specificity, here's a fairly readable description of how it's calculated.
  http://www.onderhond.com/blog/work/css-specificity

And lastly, css-d (aka css-discuss):

- Wouldn't it be nice to have a group of knowledgeable CSS experts that you could go to and ask questions? Wouldn't it be nice if everyone could ask them questions? Wouldn't it be nice if everything they'd been asked for the last seven years could be searched? And wouldn't it be nicest of all if their best tips and tricks were added to a wiki? That's css-d.
  http://www.css-discuss.org

extra bits

validate your css p. 120

- Don't forget to validate your XHTML: Your CSS validates just fine, but you still have a problem on some (but not all) pages? One possible reason: the XHTML on the pages doesn't validate, causing them to render in quirks mode. That's when browsers shift into a mode that is more forgiving of poorly formed XHTML. Validate your XHTML at http://validator.w3.org/, and you're more likely to get stable CSS rendering.

- Know which errors you can ignore. As seen in the example shown, you don't have to worry about the −vendor properties, because they are used for browser-specific enhancements.

get debugging tools p. 121

- There is a version of Firebug, called Firebug Lite, that you can download from the same site and use with Internet Explorer, Safari, and Opera. It's a little harder to use and less powerful than Firebug in Firefox, but it's still good to have.

debug css p. 122

- Test multiple browsers: the general rule of thumb here is to start with the most standards-compliant browser you have (generally Firefox or Safari; either platform), make it work, and then add in workarounds for the browsers still having trouble.

learn more about css p. 124

- These links are current as of when this book went to the printer. However, it's common for Web pages to move or become obsolete, so we'll keep an updated list of links online at http://www .dori.com/css/links.html.

- Keep an eye out for outdated information about CSS. There's a lot of it out there. In the early days, there was so little solid information about what worked that everyone wrote up everything they could to help out everyone else. Now, however, it's unlikely that your site truly needs hacks to work around problems with long-obsolete browsers such as Netscape 4, or IE 5 for Mac or Windows.

index

index

index